WHY ANIMALS ARE

SMARTER THAN US

WHY ANIMALS ARE

SMARTER THAN US

WE'VE GOT THE PROOF

The publisher

SMARTER than JACK Limited (a subsidiary of Avocado Press Limited)
PO Box 27003
Wellington
New Zealand
info@smarterthanjack.com
www.smarterthanjack.com

The creators

Text layout: Dominic Hurley
Cover design: DNA Designed Communications Limited
Cover photograph: © Rachael Hale Photography (NZ) Ltd 2004. All
    rights reserved. Rachael Hale is a registered trademark of Rachael Hale
    Photography Limited
Contributing veterinarian: Dr Andrew Whiteside BSc DipSc (Dist) BVSc
Research and writing of unattributed passages: Carolyn Weston,
    Jenny Parkin and Hayley Stent
Scenario drawings: Rhona Beesley of Action Direction Limited,
    www.actiondirection.com
Creator of SMARTER than JACK® medal: Simon Cosgrove
Story typing: Hayley Stent
Proofreading: Vicki Andrews
Compiler: Jenny Campbell

The distributors

Humane society partners: Royal New Zealand SPCA, RSPCA Australia,
    Canadian Federation of Humane Societies
Distributor in Canada: Publishers Group Canada
Distributor in Australia: Wakefield Press
Distributor in New Zealand: Addenda
Distributor in the United Kingdom: Airlift Book Company

The legal details

First published 2004
ISBN 0-9582457-5-4
SMARTER than JACK® is the registered trademark of Avocado Press Ltd
Copyright © 2004 Avocado Press Limited

Contents

Thanks to you!

This book really belongs to everyone who has known or read about a smart animal. Many talented and generous people have had a hand in its creation. This includes everyone who submitted a story, the people who gave us constructive feedback on earlier books and cover design, and those who participated in our research and helped us make this book even better.

The teams at the Royal New Zealand SPCA, RSPCA Australia and the Canadian Federation of Humane Societies, and their participating member societies, assisted us greatly. They, including the media, helped to get the need for stories and the book known.

Dr Andrew Whiteside wrote the thought-provoking foreword and provided valuable insights, DNA Designed Communications Limited designed the cover, Rachael Hale Photography Limited provided the beautiful cover photograph, Rhona Beesley created the humorous cartoon images, Simon Cosgrove designed our new SMARTER than JACK medal, Carolyn Weston, Jenny Parkin and Hayley Stent helped coordinate all the entries and wrote all unattributed passages, Vicki Andrews did the proofreading and Dominic Hurley did the typesetting. Thanks to bookstores for making this book widely available to our readers.

Lastly, I cannot forget my endearing companion, Ford the cat. Ford is now 11 years old and has been by my side all the way through the inspiring SMARTER than JACK journey.

Jenny Campbell
Creator of SMARTER than JACK®

Creating *Why animals are SMARTER than US*

We've always thought animals were smarter than humans and now we've got the proof!

This is a heart-warming and humorous book of true stories about exceptionally smart animals. After reading it you'll be convinced that animals can read minds, sense the paranormal, foretell the future, sense distant intentions, navigate without maps, fix their own medical problems and communicate in mysterious ways. Humans, of course, cannot do these things!

You'll be amazed at the abilities of the animals in these anecdotes, from house pets to farm animals to wild creatures! Have you ever wondered how your dog knows you're thinking of taking her for a walk, or seen your cat meow at an invisible visitor? Or maybe you've marvelled at the way salmon can find the exact stream they were born in, after years in the ocean. In this book you'll read these and many other true stories about smart animals. You'll start to realise that we aren't as 'superior' as we thought we were!

Alongside the many amazing and interesting facts and anecdotes that we have researched for this international edition are numerous true stories

You may be wondering about the charming 'animal versus human' cartoons – animal lover Rhona Beesley from Action Direction created them. Action Direction specialises in communicating safety messages that are relevant and current in today's complex society. The combination of pictures and words in safety material ensures that all nationalities and ages can understand the message without the need for multiple translations. Visit www.actiondirection.com.

submitted by readers. Profit from sales will help humane societies around the world in their admirable quest to improve animal welfare.

Since 2002 the popular best-selling SMARTER than JACK series has helped raise the equivalent of US$105,000 for the Royal New Zealand SPCA and RSPCA Australia with the first three books. In 2004 the first North American edition was out in Canada.

The future of the SMARTER than JACK series holds a number of exciting books, with new 'country' editions including the United Kingdom, and new editions about various types of smart animals including cats and dogs.

If you've had an amazing encounter with a smart animal we'd love to read about it. You may also like to sign up to receive the SMARTER than JACK Story of the Week for a bit of inspiration. And don't forget about the free SMARTER than JACK gift pack. See the back of this book for more details or visit www.smarterthanjack.com.

We hope you enjoy **Why animals are SMARTER than US** – and we hope that many animals and people benefit from it.

Foreword: *Be smart like animals*

 I have been a sole practice veterinarian at the Redcliffs Animal Medical Centre in Christchurch, New Zealand for 12 years, working mainly with small animals. I have also pursued a professional curiosity by letting it be known that I treat wild animals for free. Inevitably the work has led to an abundance of stories, ranging from the amusing to the enraging, from the bizarre to the sad, with the associated rollercoaster ride of emotions that they all bring. More than a few of the animals I have worked with have proven themselves to be smarter than the average human!

So it is with great pleasure that I find myself involved with this book. I am sure the variety of stories will interest all and show you that we may not be the smartest after all. I know you will find it difficult to put down! Working with animals has given me a great love and respect for them, and without their antics – some smart, some occasionally not – the journey through life would be very dull and empty. Also, the house would be far too clean and the garden too manicured!

Many of the stories will get you thinking, and will hopefully encourage you to give the creatures around us more credit. Most animals have kept in tune with their environment and play their part in the interwoven nature of this earth, interacting intimately with its continual changes. Many of us humans, I feel, have become too manipulative and invasive, destroying this delicate balance. It's time for us to take a lesson from animals – get smarter about caring for our fellow creatures and our environment.

So go on, make a change, plant a tree and encourage the wildlife – every little bit helps, and after all it's the only earth we have!

Dr Andrew Whiteside
Redcliffs Animal Medical Centre

1

Smart animals read our minds

What difference would it make to your life if you could read other people's minds? Would men still seem to come from Mars and women from Venus? Maybe you could even understand what your adoring pet's eyes were trying to tell you.

Many animals have an uncanny knack of seeming to know just what it is we are thinking, as the following stories will show.

A terrific tortoise

I am the proud owner of a beautiful little tortoise called Trudy. She is so sweet. My husband Peter is not quite so enamoured with her but kindly made her a lovely home. I feed Trudy whenever I happen to think of it, really – which leads me to the amazing discovery I made about her.

I began to notice that, as soon as it came into my head to go and find some food for her, she would appear in her feeding area. Pete did not think this possible, and said I was either imagining things or had finally gone mad! But I ran experiments on her by feeding her at even more erratic times of the day or evening.

As soon as I decided that I would feed her and began to think about what I would fetch for her, sure enough, out she came to the feeding area. Pete spied on her, and had to agree that she would begin to come out to the feeding place before I even got to the kitchen. I made sure that he was witness to this behaviour on many occasions in order to well and truly prove the point. She would even wake from a sleep and come out of her little 'bedroom' at the moment that I thought about feeding her.

It happened every time, and even Pete now agrees that Trudy is truly a telepathic tortoise!

Chelonian enthusiast
United Kingdom

The interviewer

Years ago I wanted to work with the American Red Cross in occupied Germany. I was sent to be interviewed by a young American officer. He had a terrier sitting next to him on his desk. When I entered, the dog jumped down, gave a short bark and sat next to me.

I found this quite cute and said so. I got the job.

I later found out that the officer relied on his dog for judgement. If the dog went towards the aspirant, growled and went back onto the desk the person did not get the job. It really was amazing, and we all ended up working together for many years.

Marianne Reynolds
Australia

Andrew says: He's got the right idea – I always think animals are a great judge of character. People without pets always seem not quite right!

3

Time to go now

It was a gentle end for a wonderful friend and loved one of the family – my dear Tristram, a golden retriever of ten and a half years. He was very sick; his days had got longer and happiness shorter. This final long evening came at the end of two hard weeks during which we agonised over making the decision. His diagnosis was clear from tests at Redcliffs Animal Medical Centre. I was thorough – I knew in my heart but I wanted to be sure. He had an invasive adenocarcinoma of the bowel (bowel cancer). It eventually filled up the entire pelvic canal, which made going to the toilet very difficult.

The day had been punctuated by rain, so the evening was warm and wet. A walk down Sumner Beach was a must. When I reached for the lead, a little sparkle in his eyes recalled younger days as he eased his weary body up. The walk was very satisfying. I followed Tris along the beach as he meandered into the surf and tested all the rock pools he came across. He seemed to be keen to experience all the beach had to offer that evening. Then he decided it was time to head home, leading the way with me dragging my feet behind him.

He left behind his last pawprints on the beach. I followed my dear friend of many years and remembered the times we had shared, from times of study and struggle to busy family. He had faithfully guarded my home and family, giving back nothing but love.

Arriving home, we found that Eileen had prepared a blanket for him to rest on in the lounge. Patting the wet fur on his neck I gave him an injection of tranquilliser to relax him. He soon happily settled down and relaxed on the blanket as we showered him with praise and love. I prepared the final injection.

As I re-entered the room I could see that his eyes were restful. Gently holding his paw, still wet from the walk, I raised a vein and gently inserted the needle. He didn't even notice. Releasing the tourniquet I pushed, heavy-hearted, against the end of the syringe and the barbiturate quickly dispersed throughout his body . . . he quietly left us while we patted him gently . . . good-bye, dear friend.

He rests now under a kowhai tree in our garden, nestled in mother earth, protected by a warm blanket, curled up in peace. His memory will always remain.

Dr Andrew Whiteside
New Zealand

Sense of release

We had had Liska from six weeks old and, although I was the one who fed, walked, bathed her etc, she was a real family dog, loved by all. By the time Liska was around 13 she had become almost deaf, but with clapping loudly, patting our leg and other physical antics she understood what was required and life went on normally. The children had left home by this time and sometimes when I was busy or to give me a break my husband would take Liska for her walk. However, after many months, for some reason she suddenly started refusing to go with him unless I went as well. No matter how he coaxed her she just refused to go unless I accompanied them.

Not long after this Liska acquired a nasty lump above her eye which turned out to be cancer. It was getting worse and very painful so we made the awful decision to take her to the vet to put her to sleep. We lived in Pauanui at the time and most things, including the vet, meant a trip over the Kopu Hill. When we got there the vet said he could give her something new to help her eye, and with this renewed hope we took her home again and proceeded with the medicine. It was only a few days after this that we realised Liska was not getting any better but was worse and in quite a lot of pain. The three of us were so miserable that we decided to go back to the vet the next day and this time do the deed.

As luck would have it, the Coromandel had a vicious storm that night which lasted a couple of days. As usually happened in such circumstances, the road over the hill was closed for two to three days which meant we could not go to the vet. By then we were all so very miserable that we decided we couldn't wait another two days and my husband would use his rifle.

He stood up and patted his leg for Liska to go with him – and Liska, who wouldn't go anywhere without me, got up, looked at me, then quietly followed him from the room. She not only knew what was going to happen, she welcomed it.

Faye North
New Zealand

Forward-thinking

My Uncle Jack was a farmer and had two sheep-dogs to assist him. He told me that, as the years progressed in their shared work, these dogs began to take orders from him telepathically.

All that my uncle needed to do was think the commands and the dogs would do as he requested straight away! He did say, however, that he could only transfer one command at a time. Otherwise, things could go a bit haywire because the dogs only acted upon the thought in his head at that precise moment.

Uncle Jack treated his dogs in a really kindly manner and the three of them were very fond of each other. When my uncle eventually died in hospital his friend had been looking after the farm. He noticed that the dogs howled and became distressed at the exact moment, as George discovered later, of Uncle Jack's death. I feel sure that my uncle would have been thinking of them and saying his goodbyes to them as he slipped away.

Is it possible that all animals are able to transfer thoughts to each other? Without the use of words, are they *all* able to read each other's minds maybe?

Anon
Australia

Green-eyed horses

My father was a breeder of racehorses. He was a practical, no-nonsense kind of person, but he was totally convinced that his horses could communicate by telepathy.

Even when the horses were separated, in fields far away from each other, he noticed that when he fed one the others became anxious to be fed also. He began feeding them at different times of the day, and the same thing occurred. To prove the point he asked stable hands to watch while he fed one horse out of sight of the others and too far distant for sounds to travel, and on many occasions.

It was totally out of character for my father, but he truly believed that his horses were in telepathic communication with one another.

Joan
South Africa

Silent navigator

I farmed in Taranaki, New Zealand for most of my working life, and I am now 70.

One time I decided to see if I could run the farm using horses, as most of the work was done by contractors and I had already discovered that I could feed out faster using a horse – and that includes catching it and hitching it up. So I bought Gypsy, a Quarter draught mare, and although her back was broad I was able to ride her quite comfortably, having inherited a long pair of shanks from some Scandinavian ancestor.

Shortly after she arrived I discovered that one of the Jersey heifers had got in with the neighbour's Polly Angus steers. As I did not have a dog at the time, I decided to ride Gypsy.

As I was weaving my way through the steers, singling out the heifer and driving her towards the gate, it seemed to me that Gypsy was responding to my commands before I gave them. So I let the reins go slack on her neck to see what would happen and, sure enough, Gypsy was nosing the heifer through the mob towards the gate.

Gypsy had only arrived that day on my property and had never been on the neighbour's land, but she singled out the heifer and took her to the gate, which I discovered to my annoyance was padlocked.

I slid off Gypsy's back to lift the gate off its gudgeon pins, expecting the heifer to break back and rejoin the steers, now some distance away. But as she moved right to walk round Gypsy, Gypsy sidestepped to her left.

The heifer then backed up, intending to slip past Gypsy's offside, but Gypsy took a pace to the right. By this time I had the gate open wide enough to let them through, and Gypsy shunshied her into the next paddock and waited for me to close the gate and remount.

We negotiated the road gate without any problems. The heifer had learned that Gypsy was much faster than she was. My farm gate was not padlocked and I was able to open it from Gypsy's back, when once again she nosed the heifer through without any help from me.

Well, that's my story and I'm sticking to it.

Bill Fairgray
New Zealand

Guardian angels

During the year of 1997 my father George was sadly diagnosed with metastasis cancer, and unbeknown to us had only ten months left to live. This was a terrible shock for us all.

A month before he passed away, my mother and father decided to visit very close friends of theirs living in Queensland and spent two happy weeks there. During that time my mother decided to see a clairvoyant, and the clairvoyant told her that two cats would be entering the family. My mother, confused, replied, 'No, not two cats, I only have one cat at home.' The clairvoyant repeated, 'I see two cats entering the family.'

My parents returned home to Melbourne earlier than expected as my father had fallen ill due to a relapse. Only a day before that, my wife was busy in the kitchen when she heard a rather loud meow from outside (as we were just newly-weds we did not have any pets as yet). She quickly looked round and saw a little kitten staring directly at her through the French doors. She then ran to fetch me from the next room, but when we returned he was gone.

A little while later, sure enough, she heard another meow but, when I returned to the kitchen, once again, the kitten was nowhere in sight. At this stage I was wondering whether there *was* an actual kitten or perhaps she was playing a practical joke on me!

We wandered outside and followed the now faint meows until they brought us to our backyard shed . . . and wedged between the backyard fence and the shed was this cute little kitten.

We took the kitten inside the house, and throughout the whole day he was meowing very loudly and seemed a little distressed. Eventually he managed to direct us to follow him back into the kitchen and towards the French doors, as he wanted to be let out.

Later that evening before we went to bed we noticed with great surprise and delight that the little kitten had returned to the French doors, only this time there was another face next to his staring back at us – most obviously a sibling. Now, together, they were both meowing very loudly, wanting to enter our home.

Now, to you, this may not seem like a big deal – that two stray kittens had presented themselves on our doorstep – but we believe (just as the clairvoyant had predicted) that the two kittens (now called Saffi and Kai) were sent to us in our time of need. They were sent to console us over what was ahead with the passing of our father – and that they did. It was as if their purpose was solely to comfort us, being at our side at all times in our time of grief and giving us the chance to smile at their antics – for which we thank them so much.

Anyway, seven years later the cats are still happy and a complete part of our lives. These cats appeared out of nowhere, and from nowhere they are part of our family.

Truly, angels sent over to look after us.

Angelo Stathopoulos
Australia

Andrew says: I have heard many stories very similar to your experience. Animals seem to sense when they are needed to comfort someone in need. Care of an animal in need will never be a waste of time and might even prove to be a good form of insurance policy for your future!

13

One good turn deserves another

Many years ago I came across a horse who was in pitiful condition due to a prolonged period of maltreatment. I found the owner and asked if I could buy the mare. He said that she was a useless creature who needed to be whipped continuously and that she had been vicious towards him. He had decided to send her to the slaughterhouse, but he was quite happy to take money from me to purchase her instead.

She was just skin and bone, and she liked me no better than her previous owner! She was moody and strange and became very angry if I tried to come near her. She was a sorry sight. I named her Beauty – just to encourage her!

I asked various vets for advice on how to try to bring her back to good health. They all told me not to bother, it was too late. I took her to my father's stables and he agreed to try and help me. We slowly gained her trust, and she slowly gained weight. By the time three years had passed she really looked wonderful and was of a beautiful nature. I rode her often since I lived close by, and we explored miles of countryside together.

On one of our rides we came across a little stream. It seemed very shallow and was not very wide, so I urged Beauty to take me across – but she refused, rearing up and making a lot of noise. I dismounted and started off across the stream to show her that it was all right. At my first step I sank almost up to my neck in bog. I grabbed at the edge of the stream to stop myself from sinking right under. Beauty had moved way back out of danger, and could so easily have run off to the safety of my father's stables.

I called out to her to come, and gradually she came towards me. Amazingly, she started moving her head back and forth, which swung the reins towards me. I was able to grab at them, and she dragged me out of the bog and back to safety. She saved my life that day and repaid me for saving hers years before.

We enjoyed 16 years together, Beauty and I. In all that time I was the only person she permitted to ride her – even my father was not allowed to mount her. Beauty died eventually. One day I felt a pain and a heavy, pressing feeling inside my head. I went over to the stables later that day and found that she had died at the same time that I had felt that pain. A vet diagnosed the cause of death as a cerebral haemorrhage and I had known of the very moment when this had occurred.

Anon
Australia

Andrew says: We have lots of expression in our faces that animals often can read – especially animals like us who are higher on the food chain. Lower food chain animals like sheep show very little expression, as it is important to look neutral if you are sick, otherwise you could be eaten!

He knows me well

I have owned a dog for six years. How is it that he can know exactly when I am about to take him for a walk? As soon as I think of doing so, he begins to leap around in happy expectation.

I tried putting him outside and closing the doors and windows, then waiting for up to an hour before deciding to take him out. He still knew exactly when I made the decision! When I get ready to go out by myself and go to work, he does not get excited. Even when I work my one Sunday every fourth week, he knows he is not coming when he sees me get ready to leave. How can he possibly know?

Amazed by canine perception
United Kingdom

Copycat

Was it coincidence? I went for a cup of tea with my friend Susan some while ago. Her cat was hanging around. Susan showed me the bathroom, and the cat followed us there. I noticed that a tap was dripping and, before Susan left me there, I told her about this cat I'd heard of who would only ever drink water from a dripping tap in the bathroom of her owner's house. Susan laughed and said that her cat always drank very politely from her little bowl in the kitchen.

The very next day, so I heard later, Susan's cat was seen drinking from the dripping tap in her bathroom!

Well, I always thought cats were psychic . . .

Flabbergasted
United States of America

Missed appointment

I used to have a cat called Gerald. He was a huge ginger tomcat, and I loved him. He obviously wasn't quite so fond of me!

A friend rang me one day to ask if I wanted to go to a movie the following Thursday. I explained that I couldn't because I'd booked Gerald in to get him 'fixed' on that day.

But I actually phoned her back on the Thursday and accepted the invitation after all. Gerald had disappeared that morning and never came back. I believe he knew about that appointment with the vet.

Procreation is a very important factor in animal life!

The cat fixer
United Kingdom

Wild Blue makes a choice

Wild Blue was one of the most beautiful horses I have ever seen, but he lived up to his name. He had been brutally treated before John bought him, and John was the only person he tolerated. To everyone else he was just plain out-law, and he could buck more fiercely than most broncos at the rodeo. This wild, proud horse was on a violent collision course with people, yet he gave his heart to John.

John was not only a superb horseman, he had a way with horses too. How-ever, sometimes even he had to ride for his life, if Blue was in a mood to buck. We all admired his incredible riding skill, but none of us envied his place in the saddle on this writhing, twisting fury.

Then John was badly hurt, not by Blue or any other horse, but by an ATV when it rolled on him in a steep paddock and snapped his spine. From that day forward he was confined to a wheelchair that no amount of courageous effort could get him up out of.

When he came back to the station, he wanted to ride again. Paraplegics can ride and he had done so in the spinal unit. When he chose Blue everyone held their breath, but John was adamant.

He went out in his chair to catch Blue, and the horse stared at him. During the months when John was away, no one had touched the horse. Yet he let John catch him, and he sniffed at the wheelchair curiously. He nosed at John's legs and his master smiled, stroking his head and talking softly.

He brushed and saddled Blue, then led him up to the ramp that had been built so that he could mount. Blue stood like a rock as John pulled himself into the saddle. He turned, as obedient and quiet as the gentlest lady's hack. Never again did he buck or shy with John, who he knew could not ride as he had done in the past.

To everyone else Blue was just plain outlaw, but to John he had given his heart and he was truly his horse. They grew closer than ever. John needed a horse to be his legs, and Blue knew it . . .

He's still John's horse, in whichever field of paradise he roams, and John often speaks about his faithful friend. When John's time on earth is done, there will be someone waiting for him . . . a big beautiful grey horse with a proud head and a wild heart, and they will go forward into that promised land together . . .

Jenny Gregory
New Zealand

Beautiful Bella

My tale is as true as a tail that wags.

We have a beautiful golden retriever, Bella. We originally bought her from a local breeder known for breeding champions, so it was no surprise when Bella graduated top of the class when we finished her basic training in 1996.

In 1997 we introduced twin boys into our family. Apart from having to adjust to babies in bulk, we also had to quickly accept that we owned a dog whose level of awareness bordered on eerie.

At six months old our twins were at different levels of development. While Kyle was crawling and able to explore our home, Brodie was still only rolling around, playing with the toys I would put down for him.

One day I was busy doing the washing, only checking on the boys intermittently as both were happy. From where I was in the laundry I suddenly heard a very high-pitched yelp. Bella has a very deep bark so I ignored it, assuming that it was the neighbour's dog. *Yelp*. I heard it again and it seemed very close. I immediately ran through to the kitchen, thinking that Bella had somehow caught herself somewhere or was hurt. What I saw unfolding was not what I expected.

Our back sliding door mustn't have latched properly. Kyle had managed to open it and was on his way out. Barring his way was Bella – crouched on her belly just outside the back door. Her eyes were rolling up, searching the glass, apparently for me. I stood quietly and watched out of curiosity. Each time Kyle tried to move forward Bella would lift her head from her front paws and yelp, just loud enough to startle him from moving. I was soon to discover that this episode was just the beginning.

Three months later, I'd taken the babies outside to play. Kyle was walking and Brodie crawling. I stood at the edge of our pergola and watched their activities, with Bella sitting companionably beside me. Kyle, of course, was happily teetering around our entire backyard, but I began to become concerned when his attention turned to our large back shed. With a clearance of only about a metre, snakes are a constant concern for us in this area. I gave him the grace to wander away from it on his own, but he was soon heading behind it. I didn't say a thing, but thought to myself 'I'd better get him back'. Before I could even uncross my arms, Bella had left my side and was running down to the shed, only slowing to pick up a tennis ball in her mouth. I really couldn't understand what she was doing.

Bella quickly neared Kyle and, incredibly, gently pushed the ball into his tummy. He squealed with delight as he reached out for the ball, but Bella took a few steps backwards and placed the ball on the ground. Kyle turned around and reached down to grasp it, but Bella snatched it up and backed away from him again. My brain was truly trying to grasp what my eyes were seeing as I watched this performance for the next few minutes. Bella was slowly but surely enticing Kyle back towards our house. When she finally seemed satisfied that Kyle was out of harm's way, she allowed him to have the ball and calmly rejoined me.

This incident still amazes me. Bella's intention was not to play but to prevent Kyle from being harmed. Since that day, Bella has taken a very non-aggressive, protective attitude towards the boys. She often stands arrogantly between them and visiting dogs, not allowing the boys to even be sniffed by them.

As a family we actually feel blessed to have our beautiful Bella, and she is loved and appreciated for the 'work' she's done for us.

Madonna Wagland
Australia

Now you must believe that animals can read our minds!

What a wonderful world it would be if humans could do the same! Never again would parents have to guess what was making their baby cry – they would know immediately what their baby's cry meant. Surely not only men and women, but different cultures as well, would have a much better understanding of each other.

Wrong assumptions are often behind our many thoughtless or hurtful actions . . . if we could read each other's minds we would KNOW what it was that others needed from us.

Perhaps we would even treat our animals better if we could read what it was they were trying to tell us!

Smart animals can read our minds

Humans can't read minds

2

Smart animals navigate without maps

Could you find your way around a strange or foreign city without a map on your first visit? If you got lost in dense bush, could you save your life by finding your own way out?

Could you set sail for another country without any expensive navigation equipment on board? Most animals could: they have an incredible sense of direction . . . as the following stories will show.

If someone loses a loved one the person would be desperate to find them again. However, many humans would almost certainly give up the search long before the animals that you are about to read about. Without the help of modern communication equipment the searcher might well end up feeling very desperate, lonely and desolate.

Natural wonders

It was early on a fog-bound July morning in 2003, so foggy in fact that Adelaide airport was closed. I arrived at 8 am at the local lake for a mystical encounter with the fog-enshrouded waters there.

I witnessed a stunning sight through the mist as 50 ibis glided in like phantoms to alight on their usual perches in the trees. It was a surreal experience to witness these huge white birds emerging through the swirling fog banks. Simply spellbinding! The stuff of dreams. I seemed to be the only person there observing these natural wonders. Where was everyone else?

How did these amazing creatures navigate in formation through thick impenetrable fog, to find a tiny lake in Adelaide's suburbs? Not only that, but they landed with pinpoint accuracy on their trees. For all our supposed sophistication, we had to admit defeat and close our airspace. What a stunning achievement – humbling and inspiring.

Greg Blackman
Australia

Sight unseen

We had lived in Mandurah, Western Australia for about 12 months when my two sons made friends with a black Labrador cross called Kelly.

Kelly lived a few streets away and visited our place every day. She would always arrive at the front door a few moments before the boys returned home from school. Then Kelly and her owners left Mandurah to live in Perth 75 kilometres away. The boys were very sad and missed her.

One day, about three years later, we returned home to find Kelly sitting on the front doormat. We were all very happy to see each other. Kelly and her owners had returned to Mandurah and, even though they were now living three kilometres away from where they used to, she had managed to find us again. Amazing.

Kelly eventually came to live with us, and did so for another 11 years. A truly clever and beautiful dog who loved and protected our family and will never be forgotten.

Jenny Endersby
Australia

Smart animals know their way home

Humans don't know their way home

Mystery and determination

We all know that dogs are brilliant at following tracks and scents, but how about this for canine brilliance?

A little dog called Jessie, who is a collie/border terrier cross, often goes visiting the friends and relations of her owner on her own. The amazing part is, however, that on no less than 18 of these occasions she had never been walked to the houses of these people before, with or without her owner. (Jessie is a bit of a Houdini, by the way – she is not supposed to escape and go visiting in this manner.) So how does she find these people and their homes?

Jessie makes these outings in her home town of Leicester in the Midlands of England, and it is a decent sized city. One time, Jessie went to visit her owner's best friend who lived five miles to the north of Leicester. This was her cleverest journey of all because she had never, ever visited this house before – not even by car!

Mystified
United Kingdom

Fighting for his country

Early last century, during the years of the First World War, a British dog actually crossed the English Channel to reach his master at the battlefront in France.

One month after the dog's master had arrived there, he received a letter from his wife with the sad news of the dog's disappearance. The dog had left soon after her husband so she was feeling pretty lonely, no doubt. But the dog was at the side of his master before her letter even arrived! How ever did that dog manage to find him across a considerable stretch of water, and then across miles of foreign terrain? Now, that really was clever and shows incredible devotion and resolve.

A dog admirer
United Kingdom

Wartime companion

A story was recorded way back in the sixteenth century about a greyhound who travelled alone – on foot, of course – all the way from Switzerland to Paris. Maybe he fancied a bit of fun in France's beautiful capital city! His master had travelled in the normal way for those days, a coach. The greyhound did not leave until three days later, but managed to search out his master, who was having a fine old time in the court of the king of France without him.

Jenny Parkin
New Zealand

The Persian cat who refused a lift

It is interesting that cats can manage to find their owners across long distances, since they do not have a dog's advantage of an acute sense of smell.

One smart Persian cat I've been told about travelled alone from California to Oklahoma. He escaped from the car when the family set off for their new home, and invited himself into the neighbours' house. He must have changed his mind about living with them, however, because after two days at their place he disappeared. Imagine the amazement of the family who had relocated when the cat turned up at their new home in Oklahoma!

How did he find his family, who had moved to a place some thousand miles away, when he had never been in that part of the country before? Mind you, it took him some while – 12 months, in fact! Needless to say, the family were overjoyed to see their pet safe and sound.

A fervent cat lover
United States of America

What methods could you use to find your way in places which you have never seen or heard about before?

➤ You could smell your way around, maybe? There's a distinct smell when by the sea, for instance, and I suppose you could tell if a herd of cows had passed through recently!

➤ You could find and climb high points to view the landscape ahead – provided you can find a high point, of course.

➤ You could take note of the position of the sun, and just hope that there is no cloud cover.

➤ You could follow the line of rivers or the coastline, if either of these were available.

Or you could rely on your natural sense of direction. Fine for some of us, maybe . . .

Pigeon pal

There was once a racing pigeon who stopped off for a rest one day in a back garden in West Virginia, much to the delight of the 12-year-old boy who lived there. It was wearing a tag with the number 167. The two took a fancy to each other, and the bird gave up his career as a racing pigeon and became the boy's pet.

Some time after this, the young man needed surgery and was sent to a hospital over 100 miles away from his home. He was required to remain in the ward for some days after his operation to recuperate before returning home.

One night there was a snowstorm and the boy thought he could hear a strange noise at the window close to his bed. He called a nurse to investigate, and she opened the window to see what was happening. In flew a pigeon! The boy knew it would be his pet, but asked the nurse to read the number on its tag. Sure enough – it was number 167!

Sadly the bird was not allowed to stay in hospital with his mate, but there was a very happy reunion when the boy eventually returned home.

Anon
United States of America

Animals are incredibly smart in that they can manage not to get lost without the use of maps or compasses, asking a policeman or obtaining directions from the local store! Animals and birds use a variety of methods to navigate, some simple and some very sophisticated, and some animals use these skills to travel huge distances around the world.

One method that seems reasonably simple is to use the sun or the stars – visual clues. Of course the sun moves across the sky during the day, and so it must be the actual position of the sun which provides the information. Flying creatures – including birds, bees, wasps and butterflies – and even ants use this method of navigation.

But what happens when cloud obscures the sun? Birds and insects are still able to find their way by using the position of the sun, using polarised light. The vibrations of the light waves from the sun then become limited to one plane, instead of shining in all directions as they do when no cloud is present. Frogs and toads use the North Star, Polaris, to plot direction, much as humans might do.

Worker bees use the sun to ascertain the direction of nectar in relation to their hive, working around the movement of the sun during the day. Scent plays a part as well. During the 'round dance' of the bees, the scent given off during the dance indicates the source of the food. A special pattern is made during the 'waggle dance' to show the whereabouts of the food in relation to the direction of the sun.

Birds make extremely long journeys when they migrate, and they use the visual clues of familiar features in the landscape such as rivers and coastlines to remain on course. Many other animals also use visual clues to find their way when journeying.

Water creatures use chemical changes – changes in the composition of their environment – as a method of navigation. Salmon do use the coastline to help map routes, but it is the chemical make-up of the water that allows them to recognise their own river when they return from the ocean. Salmon remain at sea for several years, so the chemical balance of their own river must remain in their memory for at least that period of time.

Chemicals also play a part in the direction of flight of male moths when they are drawn by the scent or pheromones of the female many miles away – up to seven miles in the case of the Chinese saturmid moth. Eels dwelling in Europe use the chemical content of waters to navigate when they migrate across the North Atlantic Ocean to breed. They are also aware of tiny electrical currents in the water which help them find their way and, since they also travel overland for some distance, must be able to use the magnetic field of the earth to navigate when out of water.

Andrew says: At a university up north it was found that, when animals were compared in their ability to get through a maze, humans were outsmarted by many species. One of these superior maze-solving species was the pig! They had a cheeky way of ensuring that they didn't return down the same dead end repeatedly – they marked the dead end with urine. Once a track was marked, they avoided it. Now, that's smart! I guess they avoid the void.

Smart pigeons carried the mail

Centuries before aeroplanes were invented, pigeons carried messages from place to place. Carrier pigeons were used by the ancient Greeks and Egyptians, as well as during the Franco-Prussian war of the 1870s and the Second World War. Pigeons have even been awarded medals. But New Zealand can claim the world's first airmail postage service – thanks to the work started by a small pigeon named Ariel.

In New Zealand, this transport system began with the wreck of the steamer *Wairarapa* off Great Barrier Island in 1894. As many as 135 people were killed and news of the disaster took three days to reach Auckland, which is 96 kilometres away. Nearly two years later, when the Northern Steamship Company organised a trip to the island for the victims' relatives, a newspaper reporter took Ariel with him. The pigeon belonged to Walter Fricker, an Auckland pigeon fancier.

The reporter wrote up his story and attached it to Ariel's leg with string. It took Ariel one and three-quarter hours to reach Auckland – in time for the story to appear next morning. Until then, there had been only a weekly steamer service and it would have taken people on the island 16 days to receive an answer to mail sent to Auckland.

The Great Barrier Pigeon-gram Agency started business in February 1897, but before long a similar service, led by JE Parkin, was set up in opposition. His business was later taken over by SH Howie. Even the pigeons found all this confusing at times. But their amazing work continued, and one fast bird known as Velocity held the record for speed. He did the trip in 50 minutes' flight time, only 40 per cent slower than a modern plane.

Pigeons are able to find their way 'home', but one clever bird, known as Ginger, showed that he could carry messages in both directions. Apparently, he arrived in Auckland with a message from Great Barrier Island strapped to his leg as usual. The staff were slow in giving him his food reward, which must have annoyed him as he tore the message up with his beak. He was slapped and flew off, presumably in disgust. But he was actually putting things right, as within a few hours he was back with another message.

The original pigeon post service ended in 1908 with the advent of telegraph cable.

Patricia Reesby
New Zealand

The wonder dog of Oregon

An American dog called Bobbie received honours and awards for bravery and determination and for his incredible tracking skills, and won the love of thousands. He had his photo taken and received gifts continually, and was even presented with a miniature house in which to live, with silk curtains and every modern convenience that a dog could wish for! He was on display to the public for a whole week when he was first given his special home. He wore a silver collar which was designed and given to him. His owners made a scrapbook in which to keep the hundreds of printed articles and photos he received. He earned the title of 'The Wonder Dog of Oregon'.

Bobbie's owner and his wife and two stepdaughters lived on a farm on the Abiqua River. They had owned a dog for some years called Tootles, who was a fox terrier. Then they bought an adorable little puppy, six weeks old. He was a Scotch collie, all fun and mischief. The two dogs became firm friends.

The family worked outdoors on the farm, and the two dogs frolicked around the area and shared many adventures. The family moved to other farms frequently, and the two dogs became used to exploring new areas and adapted easily. Bobbie became very good at moving animals around on the farms. This usually proved to be a harmless occupation, but on one occasion an animal objected to his 'heeling' instincts. He moved a horse back into the corral in an adept manner, but the horse showed his distaste and managed to catch Bobbie over one eye with a hefty kick, leaving a scar.

On the very next farm to which the family moved he suffered another accident. He was having a well-earned rest in the sun, and fell into a very deep sleep. He did not hear a tractor approaching, and one of his feet was run over. Fortunately, the ground was soft and he was left with a second scar rather than permanent damage.

His third scar was inflicted upon him while chasing a gopher. The rodent tried to hide in the ground, but Bobbie dug furiously to get at him, and bits of two of his teeth broke off in the battle!

When Bobbie was one year old he sadly lost his little friend Tootles, who died from a paralytic stroke. The family buried him behind the barn, with Bobbie watching and sharing the family's sorrow. At this point the family made a drastic change in their lifestyle when they bought a business – a restaurant in Silverton. Because it was felt that the life would not be good for a dog

previously allowed the freedom of running around farms, he was sold to friends who took on the farm from which they were moving. To Bobbie's family this seemed a good option, but he had an even better plan. He decided to split himself between both sets of owners, remaining on the farm during the week and taking himself into town to spend weekends at the restaurant!

At one point the family decided to take a trip out east by car. They decided to buy Bobbie back from his new owners so that he could accompany them on the journey. Bobbie was most appreciative, making the most of the journey by going off exploring alone every time they stopped for a snack. He would always be back in about an hour, excited that they were on their way again. On one occasion the mother was visiting a friend in Wolcott, Indiana and the father and Bobbie had taken the car to a filling station. Bobbie ran off

39

somewhere and did not show up after his normal hour. They drove around looking for him, tooted the horn, called and whistled – all to no avail.

By evening he had still not returned and the family began to worry. There was still no sign of him the next day, or even during the next week. They were absolutely heartbroken and stayed in the area for three weeks, longer than they had originally planned, to search the whole area, putting up signs and placing advertisements in the local paper. Not one person had spotted him. Eventually they carried on with their trip, hoping that by the time they returned to the area someone would be keeping Bobbie with them to await their return. Weeks later, when they came back through, he had still not appeared. Their holiday period over, the family returned home without him. They left copious instructions with the local community, and

left their details so that they could be contacted if he should appear.

Six months later one of the daughters, Nova, was walking along a street with a friend and thought she could see Bobbie coming towards her. She could not believe her eyes! He was in a rough state – very thin and his coat was a mess. On hearing Nova's voice Bobbie rushed to her, and in a state of frantic exhilaration was leaping up, covering her face with kisses and making excited noises. He had travelled at least 2551 miles, not including any detours he had made in the process of searching for his beloved owners. Nova took Bobbie back to her parents' restaurant, where investigation showed that the poor dog – who appeared to be Bobbie but was almost unrecognisable in his sorry state – had the three identifying scars from his farm life: ample proof, even though his incredible excitement at having found the girl was enough to prove the point!

Bobbie's toenails were worn right down and his eyes were inflamed – it had obviously been a harrowing journey for a dog on his own.

The astounding and immense love Bobbie had for his family had driven this amazing dog to travel, over all kinds of terrain, for six months until he was reunited with his family. How many humans could do the same?

Hayley Stent
New Zealand

Echolocation is a great method of navigation, used by bats to avoid obstacles and catch insects for food, and by some birds when flying in caves.

Earth's magnetic field could be described as invisible lines of force from the North Pole to the South Pole, as detected by a compass. It is thought possible that whales use this magnetic field to find their way. Various birds use it, too. For instance, emperor penguins separate from their partners when they migrate. They travel over many miles of snow-covered terrain and yet always manage to meet each other later at the new destination. (The 'penguin method' obviously works better than verbal descriptions of meeting places between human partners, which often lead to hours waiting on windy street corners in a bad mood!) There are no easily distinguishable features in a snowy landscape, so the earth's magnetic field must be the answer to their accuracy in meeting up again.

Homing pigeons and albatrosses also use this method to set the course of their flights. The answer as to how these birds can utilise the line of the magnetic field is found in the actual make-up of birds themselves, and this is borne out by the discovery of magnetite, which is a form of iron, in the brains of bees. Maybe people with a bad sense of direction should ask for a blood test to check their iron level!

Magenta

Magenta is a female spayed Himalayan sealpoint cat, now aged 18 years. We've always had an extraordinarily close and deeply bonded relationship.

In the early 1990s, my husband and I lived on a rural property some 25 kilometres south of Hobart, and Magenta, then aged six, had known no other home. My husband and I separated, and I moved to a city property on the outskirts of Hobart. I took my three cats, one of whom was Magenta, with me to this new and very different environment. All three were country cats: they knew only wide open spaces, deserted unsealed roads and low population density.

They were utterly mortified by the strange, noisy landscape into which they were now thrust, and became extremely stressed. After only days, the most highly strung of the three, Scarlett, could stand it no longer and fled. She was never recovered. Fearful that the other two would follow in Scarlett's footsteps, I drove them back to my marital home at the end of the first week. I left them in the care of my husband, with whom I believed they would feel safe. I then returned to my new city home.

That very night, my husband reported that Magenta had disappeared. Frantic, I returned to the marital home and called Magenta almost until dawn, without result. Over the next few days, I produced and distributed flyers and called on neighbouring homes, in the desperate hope that someone had seen my beloved Magenta. One week went by, then two. By the beginning of the third week I had lost hope, and the grieving process began.

Then, on the twenty-first day after Magenta had disappeared from her old country home, she arrived – exhausted and badly injured – in Hobart, a journey of some 25 kilometres. As I sat watching TV that evening I could hear the persistent distressed cries of a cat in the distance, growing rapidly closer and, as I looked round, I saw Magenta jump onto the windowsill of the room where I was seated.

Although Magenta had never seen the city house from the outside, and had been transported to and from the house by car in a covered basket, she was able to navigate a distance of 25 kilometres through towns, suburbs and heavily trafficked roads to locate me. She was severely emaciated, with worn and bleeding paws, and coughing and sneezing blood. But for 21 days she persisted in her quest to be reunited with me, and left the only home she had ever known to seek me out.

We rushed her to a vet to treat her injuries. Upon hearing Magenta's story, he remarked that in 20 years of practice he had heard several stories of cats returning to their homes, but never of a cat leaving her home to find her caretaker as Magenta had done. How did she know which direction to head in, how did she know not to give up or turn back? How had she coped with all the dangers of the journey? And how did she know when she had reached the right suburb, and the right house?

Magenta was always a remarkable personality, but this feat was extraordinary. At 18 Magenta is a fragile old lady, but she retains the amazing intelligence and fighting spirit which enabled her to survive this gruelling trek so that we could be reunited. We are both very glad she made it home.

Amanda Meadows
Australia

Now, aren't you envious of the navigational skills of these animals?

If we had them too, we would never again have to struggle with reading a map and trying to figure out just how to get to the street we're looking for. We could set off on voyages and adventures without any fear of ever getting lost. Foreign lands would no longer seem so frightening to us. We'd even feel happy about driving in some of those crazy cities in other countries!

Imagine how it would open up the whole world to us all if we could navigate like the animals in these stories.

3

Smart animals sense distant intentions

Can you sense who is ringing before you even answer the phone? Can you tell the exact moment your loved ones arrive home? Is it possible to tell whether a stranger has good or evil on his mind no matter how pleasant he appears? Many animals can even use this sense to save lives!

Message unseen

It was Mother's Day 2002. I had been out with my friend Margaret, walking my two Yorkshire terriers Peter and Molly. At that time Margaret was 70 and lived with her husband Bob. She has never learned to drive.

After our walk I was about to leave for the day. I was in the garage about to get into my car when I heard Molly barking madly. I went inside to see what all the commotion was about. Molly kept barking and trying to jump up onto the desk. She had never done this before and there was nothing on the desk that she could possibly want.

She kept jumping and jumping, and banging her nose on the drawers because she was too little to make the jump. I picked her up and put her on the desk. She stopped barking and stood over my answering machine and stared at it. She looked at me, then stared at the machine again.

It was then that I noticed I had a message. It was from Margaret, telling me that she thought Bob had had a heart attack. The ambulance was on its way and she needed me to drive her to the hospital. Thanks to Molly alerting me to Margaret's message I was there quickly. We followed the ambulance to the hospital, where Bob died later that day.

Ruth Silverwood
United States of America

What about us?

Our pets give us unconditional love, and animals are invaluable companions to many pet owners. When Christine came home one day to find that her husband had left her and she had been the unwitting victim of a marriage of convenience (her husband had just wanted to use her to get residency), she felt she had no reason to live any longer. She had loved her husband and believed that he loved her in return, and finding that she had been deceived was more than she could take. Her natural fear of death deserted her and she planned to end her life.

Christine made sure someone would look after the cats 'if anything happened to her', and readied pills and alcohol on the table. Just as she was about to take them her cats, Martha and Socks, jumped up together onto the table in front of her and sat and stared. As cat owners will know, no one can stare quite like a cat. The cats gazed penetratingly at her. Christine could feel their love and support warming her heart, and could almost hear them thinking *But what about us? Don't you want to stay with us? We love you, and we want you to stay!*

She stared back at them, and realised that in her grief and confusion she had forgotten something very important – that she was loved. She got rid of the alcohol and the pills, and started living life afresh with her loyal and loving companions. And she found herself happier and more complete than she had ever been before.

Anon
United States of America

Telepathic contact

I work in advertising, and my job calls for a lot of commuting to locations throughout the United Kingdom. My dog Cody seems to know my flight schedule! Whether I'm flying in from Dublin or London, whether I've been gone hours or days, and whatever the time of day, my wife sees Cody go wild barking and turning in circles while I land at Bristol International Airport and, once the plane has landed, sit quietly looking out the window until I arrive home.

I know that some other dog owners, who are sceptical but willing to be convinced, have tested their animal's ability to sense their journey home, with a video set up to record their pet's habits. They then leave their pet at home alone, and return at a time which has not been decided before leaving and using different modes of transport – their own car, a train, walking or a taxi – to eliminate any possible clues that would involve the animal's normal five senses. In many cases, the animal moves to a front window or door at the same time their owner sets out for home. The probability of that happening by coincidence is extraordinarily low. As Sherlock Holmes said, 'Once you have eliminated the impossible, whatever remains, however unlikely, must be the truth!'

Bonded dog owner
United Kingdom

Patient Mulle

Back in 1935 my family owned a grey and white cat called Mulle. Every morning the cat followed my brother (14 years old) and me (10 years old) to the school bus stop. After school the cat was already sitting patiently at the same stop to accompany us home. If we did not arrive at the same time, she came back twice to pick us up separately. We could never figure out how Mulle knew when we would arrive, since she spent the whole morning at home.

This cat was not just our companion but also a comfort to the whole family. The fascists had arrested our father, and our mother was very unhappy. Every time she cried, Mulle jumped on her lap, put her front paws around our mother's neck, leaned her head against our mother's and purred. This was so cute and funny that we all had to laugh despite the sadness. With her antics, Mulle did manage to light up our gloomy everyday life.

Later on, Mulle had a litter of black kittens in our kitchen. One day she disappeared, which was very unusual. We looked everywhere, but could not find her and started to feed the kittens with a bottle. Suddenly, we heard a faint meow outside and went to investigate. It was Mulle, who was badly injured. She had dragged herself all the way home, using only her front paws. Despite her pain, the poor animal managed to crawl home to be with her kittens and maybe her humans. We shed many tears about our brave cat.

I am 78 years old, but I shall never forget our Mulle.

Translated from a story by Renate Bàhnisch
Germany

Smart animals know who's calling

Humans don't know who's calling

Caller ID

My workmate Jean and her husband Gordon don't need caller ID, they have Buster! If Gordon calls home, Buster races for the phone and paws at it, sometimes tipping the receiver out of its cradle and meowing into it! No matter what the time, or how far away the call is coming from, Buster *knows*. He only ever reacts this way if Gordon is on the other end of the line – all other calls are completely ignored!

Maggie
United States of America

On my way

My mother's Siamese cat called Toby seems to have a psychic bond with her – he always knows when she's coming home. No matter whether she's leaving early or working late, he'll miraculously arrive at the doorstep as soon as she gets home. My dad and I have noticed that if she calls to say she's coming home, her faithful Siamese friend will immediately jump up to the window and keep watch, tail twitching!

Anon
United Kingdom

She knew!

Something strange happened several years ago. My little mongrel dog Trixie was a friendly, good-natured animal and loved people. Visitors always received a warm welcome – until something very strange happened.

I wanted some renovations done to my home and phoned a builder who had been recommended to me. He said he'd call in on his way home, about 6 pm. When he knocked on my door, Trixie went berserk. She flew against the door, barking and growling and made it very clear she was not prepared to let him in. My son had to drag her away and shut her in his room, where she whined and scratched at the door all the time I was talking to the builder. I was at a loss to understand her strange behaviour, as he was a polite, professional young man.

When the man had well and truly gone we let Trixie out. She came out of that room with every hair on her neck standing on edge, then searched every inch of the house and the grounds to make sure he was really gone. All that evening she lay and watched the front door. The next day she was her old self again.

This all happened on a Monday. The following Monday I read the paper and the story was on the front page. This nice young man had gone on a rampage over the weekend and shot a woman and her child, then turned the gun on himself.

How had Trixie known about a murder before it even happened? When he came to my house the man himself could not have known what he was going to do, or why would he have bothered coming looking for work?

I often ponder over this and can find no explanation.

Stella Greyling
Australia

Try asking yourself the following questions:
➤ Would you like to know the exact time to put the dinner on for your partner, who is often late home from work?
➤ Would accurate daily weather forecasts be useful in your daily routine?
➤ Would it be helpful to know if you were about to have a nasty accident?
➤ Are you able to judge whether that new next-door neighbour is a trustworthy person?

Sensing

When my father was working out of town, he sometimes called us at home in the evening. A minute before the phone would ring our cat would become agitated and sit by the telephone. If he caught a train home when the job was finished, the cat would sit down outside the front door for half an hour before he arrived.

None of this happened as a regular pattern, but somehow the cat knew exactly where he was and what he was doing.

Janice
United Kingdom

A cat's tale

This is the story of a remarkable cat. It was told to me by a young woman in 1962. I have no way of proving its authenticity, but I have no reason to believe it was anything other than an honest account of events either. I was 11 at the time and I remember how the shivers ran down my spine at the dramatic conclusion of the story. I have given the characters fictitious names because my memory is not clear about them.

According to Meg, as a child she had lived with her parents and sisters on a farm on Waiheke Island. One night Meg's mother Mary put the girls to bed and prepared to stay up and wait for her husband to return home. He was overdue from a trip to the village. She sat beside the coal range and kept the fire going while she did some mending. The family cat was snuggled asleep in front of the hearth. He was a nondescript tabby tomcat called Cuddles.

The family lived a fairly isolated existence with few luxuries. There was no telephone and the only form of entertainment was the wireless.

As Mary listened to the wireless she became increasingly anxious as the wind began to howl and the rain beat a steady rhythm against the windows. Mary found herself talking to Cuddles in an effort to quell a deep sense of foreboding. 'Where on earth can he be, Cuddles? He should have been home ages ago. Maybe the horse has gone lame or he's stopped to have a few beers with the boys.'

The cat pricked up his ears and raised his head at the sound of her voice, then returned to the serious business of sleeping. Another hour passed and still John had not returned home. Mary put her mending away and decided to go to bed. She reassured herself that John must be sheltering from the storm at one of the neighbours', waiting for it to subside before riding home.

She was about to turn off the kitchen light and make her way down the hall, when she heard the sound of horses' hooves galloping up the dirt track leading to the house. With a sigh of relief she turned back into the kitchen and hurried to the door to raise the latch. As she reached out to touch the latch the cat let out an unearthly mewing sound and leaped at her hand, scratching her fingers viciously. Mary jumped back in shock and sucked at her wounded fingers, eyeing the cat in amazement at the sudden attack.

Cuddles continued to mew and guard the door. His fur stood up straight along his spine, and his eyes were wide and wild. Mary tried a second time to get near the latch and again the cat pounced,

but this time she managed to withdraw her hand in time to avoid getting clawed. The sound of the hooves had stopped and she edged towards the window to peer out. She could just make out a figure astride a horse waiting at the gate. Then the rider urged the horse to turn and galloped back down the track away from the house.

Mary couldn't be sure whether it was John or someone else because it was too dark. Whoever it was, they had decided not to come in. She returned to her chair beside the range, puzzled and shaking her head at the strange behaviour of her cat. Cuddles continued to patrol the back door, but he had ceased mewing and his fur was returning to normal. 'What's wrong with you, you stupid animal, what do you think you're doing?' Mary scolded him.

She went to the sink to wash her hand and apply some salve to her fingers. The cat slunk back to his favourite spot beside the range, curled up and went to sleep.

Another hour passed before Mary heard a horse galloping fast up the track. She quickly went to the back door and opened it, and the cat made no move to stop her. This time it was definitely John; she watched as he tethered the horse beneath a tree and ran towards her.

'Are you okay, Mary?' he asked as he hugged her. 'Yes, I'm fine, John,' she replied, 'but where have you been all this time?' Once inside the warm kitchen with the door closed, John began to explain.

'Some bloke went berserk with an axe. Anyone who opened their door to him got chopped up. Me and a few of the boys took off after him. He attacked about six people. We tracked him down but it took ages to finally corner him. Don't worry, he's locked up at the settlement now. Riding back home I suddenly thought he could've come here. I was terrified in case he'd attacked you or the girls.'

Mary's eyes were wide with horror and she had to take a deep breath before speaking. 'Did you ride up here about nine o'clock to warn me?' she asked, her voice trembling.

'No, we were searching on the other side of the island about that time.'

'Oh John, it must have been him, there was someone on a horse waiting at the gate!'

Then she told him about the cat and how he had stopped her lifting the latch. They both agreed that the cat had saved Mary from serious injury, perhaps even death, that night. Needless to say, from that day on, Cuddles the cat was hailed as a hero.

Carole Hull
New Zealand

Now you must be convinced that animals can sense distant thoughts!

Wouldn't it be great if you could tell it was just a salesman ringing in the middle of your family dinner and you could leave the phone unanswered!

Or if you knew exactly when to time the hot meal for guests arriving from far away?

Or, far more seriously, whether the person on the other side of your door was safe or dangerous even before you opened it?

Wouldn't life be simpler if you too could sense distant thoughts?

4

Smart animals are natural doctors

Could you diagnose all your own illnesses? And if you could, would you be able to find exactly what you needed to treat them? Would you be able to keep yourself, and maybe even others, well without having to study medicine for seven years? Many animals can do just that!

Imagine you are a female (that's if you're not one, of course). You believe you may be pregnant and you live in a desolate place where there are no doctors. What could you do to test yourself?

Would you:
➤ wait and see for a few months?
➤ wait to see if you feel nauseous frequently?
➤ go into a trance and reach your inner being to find the answer?
➤ read this book (which you would certainly have taken with you!) to find the answer to your problem?
➤ ask the advice of an animal?

Andrew says: We used to have a lovely golden retriever called Tristram and he had an amazing ability to detect if someone was pregnant. He would give the game away, even if the person was not ready to make it public knowledge! Well, all animals (us included) release phero-mones. It would seem that during pregnancy women are sending messages to their pets, who often respond – helpfully!

Cockroaches for dinner

I have a female cat who is never really interested in hunting. She has never caught a (live) bird in all her life.

When I fell pregnant, however, things changed. She started bringing little 'gifts' into my bedroom. Giant cockroaches, mice, moths, lizards and one day even a partially decomposed bird. She obviously thought I needed extra nourishment while I was pregnant. As soon as I gave birth, the little 'presents' stopped.

How did she know I was pregnant? Amazing.

Janelle Hayes
Australia

Pregnancy test

It all started on September 20, 1984. My mother's chihuahua woke me up as she was about to give birth, so I sat up to help in the delivery. She had three pups: Wombi, Bandi and Sheila.

My fiancé at the time (now my husband) and I chose to keep Bandi, and my parents kept the other two pups. My fiancé and I were married in March 1985 and this was the only time we were apart from Bandi – which was for a week. Anyway, we settled into everyday life at our house, with Bandi to oversee that everything was in place and kept that way.

After a few months, it became obvious that Bandi knew more than we thought. She knew when I was pregnant before I did. I know this because she always slept on our bed by my feet, but when I became pregnant she would suddenly start sleeping by my tummy and, sure enough, each time I would find out I was pregnant (this happened five times).

She would always be the first to greet the new arrival with a kiss when they came home for the first time, and she was always loving, gentle and patient with them.

I am writing this as I contemplate my first Christmas without Bandi in 19 years, as we had to have what we consider one of our children put to sleep in October 2003. Life will never be the same.

Jacqui Bache
Australia

63

Test time!

Right – let's see how you would manage on your own in the wilds. Imagine that you have been eating huge amounts of food (assuming that you have been able to find enough plants and suitable animals to catch and eat in order to eat huge amounts!) but still feel continually hungry. You assume that you have a parasite in your intestine. Left to your own devices would you:

- ➤ drink lots of water?
- ➤ put yourself on a fast?
- ➤ try to find a type of food that the worm didn't like and eat that, so that it would leave of its own accord?
- ➤ find something to eat that tasted really bad and was rough and prickly?
- ➤ forget what's on top of the earth and dig down to find a cure – some yummy roots, maybe . . .

Okay, you've managed to evict that pesky parasite – wonderful! But now you've picked up a nasty tummy bug. I wonder what you could do about that. Should you:

- ➤ eat some grass?
- ➤ try that fasting again?
- ➤ drink yet more water?
- ➤ swallow some stones?
- ➤ grind up stones and swallow the powder?
- ➤ eat some hair?

Now read on to see if you might have found a cure.

Smart animals fix their own itches

Humans make their itches worse

The perfect medicine

Henry, a chimpanzee from a national park in Tanzania, was watched eating some rough, sharp-pointed and nasty-tasting leaves of *Aspilia rudis*, which is a variety of sunflower. Chimps don't usually eat these leaves. Henry folded them in the way that young children do when making a fan from paper, and then continued to fold until the leaf became a little parcel small enough to put in his mouth. He screwed up his face while chewing these leaves, as if taking some disgusting medicine. Why would he do this? His mum was not there to force him!

Well, Henry *was* actually taking medicine. The leaves are used by people who live in the same area to help stomach upsets, and have been found to contain chemicals that attack gut parasites and have antibacterial properties. Henry must have known this as well and was self-medicating.

It has also been discovered that Henry and his mates occasionally ate the leaves of about 20 other plants of equally obnoxious flavours. These leaves were later discovered to have been excreted whole, and were then studied by scientists. Amazingly, the leaves were found to have tiny worms (found in the gut of chimpanzees) wriggling around on their rough surface. If only our children were that clever – it would save a lot of tantrums!

Grizzly and black bears also self-medicate with nasty-tasting natural medicines. They chew up the roots of *Ligisticum porteri* (lovage, to people like me!). The bears swallow them to treat worms in their system or to cure infections caused by bacteria. Sometimes they spit the chewed roots onto their fur to kill parasites.

A herbalist in Suffolk, England has found an interesting remedy for purging the systems of horses. He takes their own tail hairs, dips them in honey to make them appetising and persuades the horse to eat them!

Dogs and cats are often seen eating grass, apparently self-medicating for nausea. Perhaps there is a reason for babies eating sand, grass, etc. One mother found her first-born child eating half a dead mouse! She stopped him, but maybe he knew something she didn't!

Gorillas in a mountainous area of Rwanda can often be seen eating clay. The clay was examined to find out why they might do this. It was found to contain something much like kaolin, which is prescribed to humans for stomach upsets. Elsewhere, chimpanzees have found a similar use for termite mounds – they eat the earth by the handful. Five chimps were seen having a little tea party together, munching their way through some of these turrets of earth. Some inquisitive humans came and broke up the party and ran tests on them. All five had the same ailment; they were suffering from gastrointestinal problems.

Andrew says: I think the grass must be nice and alkaline – good for settling sore tummies. Often, the grass will be used to bind up material in the stomach if it needs to be vomited up.

67

Andrew says: What awesome biological control! Don't forget, many medicines we use today were originally found in the biological environment. I'm always concerned at the way humans destroy the forests and the sea – we've only scratched the surface in our investigations into future remedies.

In Western Kenya there is a cave that has been getting larger and larger over the years! This is not due to weather conditions or even general wear and tear. Elephants – that's the answer! The local elephants have been mining. It is not an easy cave to reach, and many have sadly died in the attempt. Those who do succeed use their tusks to dig. They then grind the soft rock up with their teeth and eat it.

Elephants normally eat plants, and some of these contain toxins. The rock from the cave helps their metabolism to deal with the toxins since it contains huge amounts of sodium. This is another case of self-medication. The rock was also found to contain calcium and potassium.

Some cattle lick clay. They dig with their feet to get at it with their tongues.

Perhaps we could learn something from all of these examples. Before we go out for a night on the town, maybe we should do as the animals do and line our stomachs first!

Right – a nice plate of clay before we go out from now on? Well, maybe not.

I watched in horror . . .

My shih-tzu Buttons was about to have her first litter.

The first and second pups were born normally, but when the third pup arrived it was floppy and lifeless. I didn't know what to do and tried to pick it up to stimulate its breathing and movement, but Buttons was agitated if I went near it. I wanted to remove it from her but she was determined not to let me touch it.

Oh well, I thought, it seems to be dead and maybe she needs to see that for herself. I let her take control and the next thing I saw was beyond belief. My husband – an ambulance officer – was another witness and I was glad not to be the only person to see Buttons' next move.

She picked up the lifeless pup in her mouth, by its head, and I watched in horror. My first thought was that she was going to bite its head off. It was too late to intervene. But then she started to puff in and out very deeply and purposefully, with the pup's head still in her mouth. The pup started to move and then wriggle and Buttons let it down into the whelping box.

We humans get trained in this procedure but it was already in Buttons' instincts. We thought her pup would never be a show dog, but some time later we took him to the National Dog Show where he won Best of Breed, topping it off with Non Sporting Puppy in his group.

Mary Main
New Zealand

That itchy feeling

Ever had that horrible itchy feeling? Animals have that problem too, of course, and the first that come to mind are monkeys. I'm sure you've all seen films of monkeys looking through each other's fur and picking out pesky little creatures! In Costa Rica, some monkeys pick parts of plants to avoid this problem. They use leaves from 'cake bush' and old man's beard and seed pods from sloane ternifola to rub on their fur, which helps to repel insects and stop allergic reactions and disease from bites. Clever! As a bonus, the spiky pods are used for combing out any parasites the monkeys may have in their coats.

These monkeys also use a plant of the chilli family to rub on themselves to deaden pain. (This is interesting since rubbing your eyes after preparing chilli for a curry will inflict much pain!) Others rub their fur with millipedes, which kills off certain bacteria and other more harmful insects.

'Anting' is a similar process for some birds. They actually choose to lie on top of an anthill so that ants will creep all over them and get into their plumage. Yuck! Formic acid is then secreted there, which helps to kill off lice, mites and bacteria. Monkeys and birds obviously don't have hang-ups about insects crawling all over them like some people do!

Sheep on farms often need to be dewormed every few months. Wild sheep (yes, you've guessed it) manage very well without this process. They are troubled with few parasites. They stay healthy and have good muscle tone but are also lean. Wild boar can remain happy and lead active lives even when infected with swine fever. Wild deer have energetic long lives while infected with tuberculosis. These animals could probably offer some helpful and cost-effective suggestions to farmers.

Wild animals are less burdened by parasites, as they often have a large area to roam in and smaller herd sizes. Farming research found that by increasing the number of stock in a paddock you increase the production for that paddock. However, by doing so, individual animals are more likely to get heath problems as they are more stressed. We need to be smarter with animal husbandry!

Getting drunk or 'stoned'

Getting drunk or high on drugs is not socially acceptable for humans in many circles, but did you know that some creatures get drunk?

Elephants come at top speed to partake of decaying marula trees. They can smell the fermenting fruit from a distance of ten kilometres. One theory is that they get drunk to de-stress. It seems that, given access to alcohol, elephants eat twice as much of the 'bad' fruit than at other times. I wonder what the researchers did to stress the poor creatures and drive them to drink.

There is even a type of sheep that likes to dabble in narcotics. Bighorn, who live in the Canadian Rockies, go through great difficulty and danger to get at a nice meal of a type of narcotic lichen which grows there.

Birds called Bohemian waxwings are partial to slightly fermented rowan berries. Apparently, they are often found to have fallen off their perches after eating these. Huge numbers of the poor wee birds are found dead on the ground in great heaps. What a way to go!

One expert on animal life seems to think that animals need a boost now and again. It may well be true that their brains benefit from an occasional dose of some potent neurochemical. Maybe this is also true for human beings?

Drinking problem?

Many people do not consume alcohol, either because of personal beliefs or because they simply do not like the taste. Some people are left with a horrendous headache if they partake of more than the odd one or two! But now we know that even animals and birds like to indulge in this pastime. If it caused nasty after-effects for them also, surely they would be sensible enough never to touch the stuff! Those birds who fell off their perches? Well, maybe they were 'workaholics' who really needed a rest!

It could well be the many chemicals or additives introduced to our modern brews that cause the nasty after-effects. If we took a tip from animals and birds and used only natural products, maybe people would not suffer from the occasional sociable glass of wine. Maybe we would even benefit from the odd tipple and feel better instead of worse.

First aid

Teachers – especially those who teach young children – often feel that they should regularly attend courses in first aid in order to become confident in treating other people's little darlings! How can animals know what to do just by pure instinct?

It makes some of us wonder about doctors saving the lives of accident victims, for example, who are left with very little quality of life. Should we walk off and leave them instead? An animal always seems to see into the future, knowing which of the litter to leave for the benefit of the siblings, and so on. If only we could have confidence in our instincts as modern-day human beings!

Murphy's return

Murphy was a mischievous terrier cross, who lately had been going off on doggy wanderings without his owner. This led to the inevitable decision by the owners to get him neutered in the hope that it would reduce his excursions. We neutered him at the clinic in Redcliffs. All went well and he was discharged. His stitches were due to come out ten days later.

The surgery seemed to help as, after it, he didn't run away as before. Except, one day, who did we find wagging his tail at the front door waiting to be let in . . . Murphy, looking very pleased with himself! It was exactly ten days later and his stitches were due to come out. After removing his stitches we rang his surprised owners to come and pick him up. Other than for vaccinations, when he comes with his owners, we have not had any further visits!

Dr Andrew Whiteside
New Zealand

Wouldn't the world be a different place for humans if we had the same instincts as animals for keeping ourselves healthy?

Even though we are lucky enough to have marvellous doctors and health professionals, imagine how much easier it would be if we could just treat ourselves. We could not only figure out what was wrong with us and what we needed to take to get better, but we could even prevent illness in the first place!

Billions of dollars spent all over the world on hospitals and expensive drugs could instead be used to help those who are starving.

Wouldn't that be amazing!

5

Smart animals sense the paranormal

Do you sometimes get a creepy feeling in an old house? Would you like to know for sure whether ghosts are 'real' or not? Wouldn't you like to be able to see whether the dead truly can communicate with the living?

See if these stories can convince you that animals can sense those on the 'other side'.

Do you think animals believe in ghosts? It seems that they do, because the only other possibility is that our pets have a brilliant sense of humour and enjoy pretending to sense the paranormal and scaring their owners just for fun!

If you like to feel a tingle up your spine, maybe this chapter should be read after dark when you are all alone on a stormy night, so that you will feel the full benefit of these eerie tales!

Where's Gran?

My German shepherd Shelley and I always visited my parents, who lived in a hostel. She always led me to the door of their room and lay beside my mother's chair during our visits. She was two years old when my mother died.

I was passing the cemetery a month or so later and decided to visit my mother's grave. I said to Shelley, 'Where's Gran?' She went straight to my mother's grave and lay down beside it.

I later realised that there were fresh flowers on the grave which had been placed there by my father the day before. I believe Shelley followed his scent – but she certainly made the hair stand up on the back of my neck.

My father has since died and is buried with my mother, and Shelley still knows where their grave is, even though other graves now surround it.

Sancia Wheeler
Australia

Smart animals sense passed lives

Humans can't sense passed lives

An invisible guest

I was watching TV one night when I heard footsteps above me, though I was home on my own. My cat and dog both looked up, and their eyes tracked the sound as our invisible guest walked down the stairs and through the kitchen to the living room. I was most disappointed that I couldn't see what they apparently could, only hear the footsteps.

Feeling left out
United States of America

A soul beneath the earth

When my family lived in Maine we had two pets, a cat and a dog. One day when my mother (a nurse at the local hospital) was leaving for an early shift, she found the cat had been hit by a car outside our house and killed. She buried the cat in the back-yard and set off for work.

Later that morning, the dog went to the spot where Mom had buried the cat and lay down. It wasn't one of his usual spots to lie, being shaded by a big tree all day. But, every day until we moved from that house many years later, he visited the grave site and lay there for at least a few hours.

The dog had been shut indoors when his play-mate was buried and was very likely asleep at that early hour, but he seemed to sense the location of the cat's final resting place, and was drawn daily to be close to him.

An awed animal lover
United States of America

Reduced to a nervous wreck

My friend Ron and his dog Sarge, a sturdy boxer, were exploring an office building which had been abandoned since the 1950s. Sarge was having a ball, running and sniffing, until suddenly he stopped and stood stock-still, staring along a corridor. His hackles rose and he was quivering as though cold, but when Ron bent to pat him he felt warm enough.

Then, from the far end of the hallway, Ron could hear the click-clack of a typewriter. He went to investigate, but Sarge refused to move forward another step. He searched the entire floor, but could not find the source of the sound. Ron gave up his search and turned to leave the building.

As soon as the door to the stairwell was opened Sarge scrambled down the four flights of stairs to the ground, his claws skittering and scratching on the concrete steps. He waited for Ron at the door leading outside, barking at him to hurry up and scratching at the door. Once they were outdoors he relaxed somewhat and his hackles dropped, though he stayed behind Ron as though keeping himself between his master and some unseen danger.

As they walked away from the building, Ron could still hear the faint sound of the typewriter. He felt somewhat shaken – his usually fearless companion

Andrew says: I find that some buildings or areas give me the creeps – is that our version of what some of our pets experience? Recently my father passed away. The day after my father's wake, our dog Pippa, a cute scruffy border terrier, suddenly started barking at an empty chair in the lounge where we were all gathered. It felt like my father had just popped in to check on us. Pippa has never barked at the chair again.

had been reduced to a nervous wreck by something he had encountered in that building, something Ron had not even sensed until the sound of typing reached his ears.

A creeped-out dog owner
United Kingdom

They seemed to be racing along a predestined path

I was very excited with my first horsey 'job' as an adult. I can still feel the apprehension and pride as I walked my horse onto the old Southall property and into their stable yard to prepare for the holiday camp with horses I was to lead. It didn't concern me that the Southall property was rumoured to have a resident ghost, even though it did have its own family graveyard.

The rambling old house had been built amid a granite rock outcrop and rooms grew out of rocks, on top of rocks and in some cases under rocks. For some it was an architectural masterpiece, and no doubt a nightmare for the more discerning eye. I'd loved every square inch of it from afar and relished the thought of spending a few nights there.

The family had six horses between them, and a couple of their friends had brought in horses for the camp. Children were lined up, food and kit-bags checked and, once goodbye kisses to parents had been given all round, we began our horse camp. We slept in a long-deserted wing of the house and were self-sufficient in cooking and stable management. We cooked over an open fire, as big an adventure for the children as it was for me, then a tender 17 years old.

Mornings were spent cleaning stables and grooming before the horses were taken out for lessons, games and rides. We returned in the heat of the day and lolled around the swimming pool built around the rocks, or in the peculiar glasshouse on top of one of the highest rocks. Its attraction was a collection of trunks full of old-fashioned horse tack, and old love letters from a man called Jack to his 'sweetheart'. While the children lovingly saddle soaped and waxed up mounds of old bridles and leathers, I dreamily read through the most beautiful love letters imaginable.

Jack had flown planes, and sent his letters from all over the world. After the loving thoughts and wishes and tales for his 'sweetheart', he always mentioned his horses. Were they faring well? How were the paddocks holding up? How were Bess and Blue Boy? The horsey names went on and on and I finally understood why the present stable yard was so huge for just six horses. The letters had been written well over 30 years before I read them. It could have been youthful innocence or cheek, but we never felt we were intruding on anyone's privacy as we sifted through Jack's horse tack and love letters.

It was while we were up in the glasshouse one afternoon that we witnessed the most astonishing sight. All ten horses had broken out of their paddock and came galloping across the fields below us, manes and tails flying, whinnying, bucking and snorting. Garden beds and seats and ponds didn't stop them. They raced through old orchards, leaping everything in their path. They were at one with each other and seemed to be racing along a predestined path, one that had not taken any obstacles into account. Their whinnying and snorting were outmatched only by the thundering of their hooves heard clearly through the glass walls.

We, in turn, leaped up as one and piled down the old stone staircase to dash off in the direction the horses had taken. As we landed at ground level there was an ominous silence.

We found ourselves heading towards the family graveyard, where we found another astonishing sight. All the horses had found themselves a spot around the wrought iron fence surrounding the graveyard, and appeared to be looking in one direction and gently snorting. As we trooped up to them, they didn't even glance our way. I approached my horse and looked in the direction he was staring.

The headstone read 'Jack Southall, died 16 December 19– in tragic accident at Cranborne Air Barracks'. I had good reason to remember 16 December as it had only been that morning that I had written it at the top of the page in my diary.

Do horses have the power and intelligence to see and hear what the human eye and ear cannot? Yes, to this day I firmly believe they do.

Wendy Roberts
New Zealand

Mysterious voices

I was reading a magazine in the living room when my blue heeler Flash started growling at the stairs which led to the lower floor. I was afraid that there was a prowler downstairs, and followed Flash down to the kitchen with a heavy metal statuette in my hand as an improvised weapon.

There was no one in the kitchen, and no sign that anyone had entered the house – the doors were still locked. Suddenly, I heard a voice coming from the heating vent which led to the basement – the voice of a small girl. Scared out of my wits, I returned to the living room and curled into the corner of a couch, while Flash stood guard at the top of the stairs, still growling.

Anon
Australia

A doggy wake

When my mother was a teenager in the early 1920s, she went to stay on a remote farm in the King Country with her Auntie Annie Grice. During the time that she was there, word came through that a brother of her aunt's had died suddenly while at a stock sale.

Findlay McDougall had lived alone on another remote farm in the Upper Retaruke district. The undertakers took him to the mortuary and later to another town to be buried, so he never returned to his farm. As he was a single man of 45 years, a neighbour looked after his stock until some decision could be made as to his estate.

About a week after his death my mother and her aunt travelled to his farm to deal with his clothes and goods inside his house. My mother was asked to take her Uncle Findlay's clothes from the house and hang them on the clothes line to air. These were clothes that had been in the house all along.

Findlay's four dogs, who were having the freedom of a run off the chain at the time, immediately went and sat under the clothes hanging on the line and began to howl. My mother said the sound was so eerie and heart-wrenching that after an hour or two her Aunt Annie and she could stand it no longer and removed the clothes back inside. Immediately the dogs stopped their howling and went voluntarily back to their kennels.

How could those dogs have known their master was dead and given him the equivalent of a doggy send-off?

Celia Geary
New Zealand

Watching someone who wasn't there . . .

I believe that animals can sense ghosts and other paranormal beings long before humans feel a cold chill or a prickle on the back of their neck. My aunt Mary related this story to me years ago, and I still find it quite chilling!

Shortly after moving into a house in Kent, Mary observed her cat behaving strangely. He would sit in the front hall staring up at the top of the stairs, and slowly move his head as though watching someone descending. Sometimes he would stare at a particular spot on the ceiling which, to Mary, looked exactly like the rest of it.

One morning, while Mary was at the breakfast table, she heard heavy footsteps pounding above her, though there was no one upstairs. The cat was flat on the floor, tail puffed up with fear, hissing and staring up towards the noise. The racket lasted around half a minute before fading. Mary went upstairs to make sure that nothing was amiss, and found the rooms empty.

Shortly after this incident she decided to sell the house, and her cat has never shown any signs of sensing anything other-worldly since leaving the house.

Chilled to the bone
United Kingdom

Do you think you could:

- ➤ guess where your best friend was buried without the help of a name plaque or headstone?
- ➤ feel bad vibes if you were about to buy a house where someone had recently been murdered?
- ➤ be able to rely on your instincts to ascertain whether there was an intruder on your property?

It seems that animals can see and feel people we think have long gone.

Wouldn't it be great if we could, too? We could know which houses to avoid buying almost straight away, as we'd sense any ghosts if they were there. Perhaps we could communicate with loved ones long gone and see how they're now faring, putting our minds at rest.

Most importantly, maybe we wouldn't fear the paranormal if we were actually able to see it.

Would that be the end of horror stories?

6

Smart animals communicate in mysterious ways

If we couldn't talk, would we be able to communicate with each other very well? Would we be able to follow detailed directions without any words being spoken or a map drawn for us?

Many different animal species can, and these stories will show just how well animals can communicate without using any language at all!

This chapter gives many examples of the way communication has evolved for different species and the incredible interaction that occurs between animals. And these are just the ones we know about!

Smart animals use natural scent to attract mates

Humans use artificial scent – with bad results!

Sweet scent

Droppings make for perfect scent markers. The European rabbit drops 800 of these scent markers every day.

The hippopotamus spreads its muck by swinging its muck-coated tail and muck-encrusted feet. This effectively marks its territory, fending off rivals.

Urine on the feet is a good tactic for creating odour signals. This fetching technique is used by some lemurs, monkeys and lorises.

Pheromones are used by female silk moths to get the males to do what they want. Airborne molecules are excreted from their scent glands, which the male can sense up to three kilometres away – if one lands on their feathery antennae. This arouses the male and he embarks on a mission to find the owner. To avoid confusion with other lustful males, the female encodes the release of her pheromones by sending out her scent in short bursts. The two moths can then find their soulmate.

Dancing bees

Many of us have no sense of direction – some of us can even get lost in a supermarket! Without supermarkets some of us would not even be able to feed ourselves adequately unless we were good at growing vegetables and had a good knowledge of wild plants. It appears that we could pick up some useful tips from bees!

Domestic honeybees live in a hive. Different bees have different jobs to do and look after each other really well, without the use of language of course. There is one fertile female queen bee, a few drones (which are male) and literally thousands of worker bees. Some of these workers are good little housewives who keep the hive clean, build wax combs and look after the young. Some go off foraging for food – nectar and pollen. Scout workers go out and find food and then come home to the hive. Later, as if by magic, other workers go out and fetch the food that the scouts found earlier.

There are special 'bee methods' of imparting knowledge about food sources. Directions are given as to how far away the food is, how good it is and in which direction to go off and find it. A 'round dance' shows that the food is quite close. Bees turn round to the left, then right, then left and so on. If the dance is wild, the food is especially good. If the food is over 75 metres away from the hive, this is shown with a 'waggle dance' – which is more complicated. It is made up of both looping and straight runs.

The speed and the length of time the bees buzz while looping indicate exactly how far away the food source is. Flight is in a straight line upwards if the food source is in the direction of the sun, straight down if it is in the opposite direction to the sun. If the food is to be found to the left of the hive the foragers indicate this by dancing to the left, and they dance to the right if the food is to be found to the right of the hive.

Have you got all that? Pretty simple really, isn't it! Anyway, it is great that bees know how to dance because many of us really love honey and luckily we can buy it from the supermarket.

A good vibration

For spiders, vibrations on the threads of their web tells them that prey has fallen into their trap, but it is also the means by which male spiders approach females without being eaten! The male will pluck at a thread of the web, sending the signal that he is about to approach.

Not only spiders communicate using vibrations, however. Insects which walk the surface of ponds make fast ripples to protect their territory from rivals and slower ripples to signal their availability for mating.

* * *

I gotta go!

I had two cats: a Siamese cat who was a bit of a 'dumb blonde' though very lovable, and a Burmese by the name of Panthera who was a little devil.

I used to bathe them for fleas, in a horrible concoction which the Burmese hated with a passion. The first bath went sort of fine. I prepared the second bath and then went to call them in. The dumb blonde came running, but the little devil was nowhere to be seen and stayed away until the next day, when the smell of the concoction had dissipated.

So the next time, I penned them up before mixing 'the brew'. As soon as Panthera smelled it he started prowling around the kitchen and yowling fit to wake the dead – an *I want to go out to the loo* type yowl.

Being smarter than the average cat, as I thought, I took no notice and proceeded with the task. I knelt on the floor, with Panthera between my knees to bathe his head before dunking his body in the tub. He managed to squirm his way out of my grasp and claw his way up my front to sit on my shoulder, where he proceeded to pee almost in my ear! He then got down with a look, *See, I DID want to go to the loo!* He did NOT escape the bath.

Boy, did I love that cat!

Beryl Fairweather
New Zealand

Hornbills heed warnings

It is widely assumed that birds can 'talk' to each other and that cows converse with other cows, sheep with sheep and so on. Well, there are some very clever birds who have learned to understand some of the 'language' used by certain species of mammals, and vice versa.

When 18 months were spent studying hornbills and Diana monkeys, it became apparent that these two varieties of bird and mammal, when living in the same area, understand each other's warning calls of approaching predators. This was proved when it was discovered that very different calls from the monkeys for two different forms of predator were clearly identified by the hornbills.

To the human ear the two calls used for approaching leopards and eagles sounded almost identical. However, when eagles approached, the hornbills ignored the monkeys' warning calls but, when leopards approached, the birds moved quickly away. Eagles are no threat to them, but leopards are able to climb trees to reach tree-dwelling birds such as the hornbill.

Jenny Campbell
New Zealand

Mozart's little helper

Have you ever noticed that common old starlings can sing two tunes simulta-neously? Most people do not until it is pointed out to them! Many people also have no idea that these amazing birds have a two-part syrinx, until it is explained to them.

Mozart kept a starling as a pet and it would often entertain Wolfgang and his friends with its singing. On one particular occasion the bird repeated some phrases from his Piano Concerto in G Major while he was composing the work. The starling changed the 'sharps' to 'flats'. Mozart decided it was an improvement and kept them in!

When his beloved pet died, Mozart held a funeral and insisted that all his friends attend. I bet the Piano Concerto in G Major was played at the service!

Jenny Parkin
New Zealand

Electricity under the sea

Some fish – such as knife fish, blue sharks, elephant fish and, of course, electric eels – use electric fields for both navigation and communication. Some can only sense the fields and some can create them. For navigation, the fish generates a weak electric field which in most species covers an area of approximately one square metre around its body and is usually less than a volt in strength. In some species (the black ghost knife fish, for example) this field is emitted in pulses, and the frequency of these pulses is used to convey information.

Bouncing sound

Dolphins send out high-frequency sounds, which bounce off objects in the water around them. Changes in the sound which comes back to them yield great amounts of information about those objects – they can tell whether any given item is a living creature or an inanimate object, whether it is dead or alive, whether it is friendly or a threat, how large it is and how fast it is moving. They can even tell how another dolphin is feeling by picking up changes in physical signals such as heart rate, muscle tension and skin conductivity.

In addition to communication and finding food, dolphins also use sonar to navigate the seas. They can tell the depth of the water, locate obstacles such as coral reefs and form mental maps of the area.

That telling echo

Do you know what 'echolocation' means? If so, you may well be a lover of seals, bats, porpoises, oil birds, whales, shrews, dolphins, tenrees or swiftlets. All of these are able to echolocate.

Bats are a good example. They fly around with their mouths wide open, and this is part of echolocating. Bats have the best hearing of any creature on earth and use ultrasonic echolocation – pitched too high for humans to even hear. When the sound 'hits' something it echoes back to them. This is how they manage to find their way around without bumping into things, and how they find food. Even the tiniest of insects cause an echo.

Scientists suspect that bats' noses have something to do with the process! Some bats echolocate as loudly as a smoke alarm (I'm glad we can't hear that), and others almost whisper.

* * *

Now you can see just how clever animals really are. They are brilliant at making themselves understood without using any words at all! Sometimes they don't even use sound to communicate; they do it with movement or smell. Imagine if we could pick up clear messages from each other just by looking or even smelling.

Perhaps we would never feel misunderstood or get involved in arguments again!

7

Smart animals foretell the future

Wouldn't it be incredible if we could sense a disaster before it happened? Imagine if we could tell when it was going to rain heavily or an earthquake was about to strike? Or what if we could sense that a storm was on its way, or even that we were about to be in an accident if we continued with our plans?

There are some humans who claim to be able to do this. Most people are sceptical of their ability in this field and assume that various methods of cheating are used. Could it be possible, however, that some of us have retained this ability from our dim and distant past when we were mere animals?

Many animals are psychic, not just for themselves but also for those they love. The following stories will surely convince even the most sceptical among us.

Premonition saved life

Phillip, a close friend of my family, was heading out on a fishing trip off the South Carolina coast with his German shepherd Jackson, who loved going out on the boat and loved to swim in the sea.

It was a gorgeous day, not a cloud in the sky, and there was a light breeze to take the edge off the heat. A perfect day to be out fishing with man's best friend . . . except that today man's best friend seemed to be feeling contrary. Jackson wouldn't move from the jetty, not even for one of the dog biscuits Phillip always carried.

Worried that something might be wrong with Jackson, Phillip unloaded his gear and headed home. Later that morning a storm warning sounded, and the wind rose; by the time the storm had blown itself out, many lives had been lost. If Jackson hadn't known the storm was coming, or if Phillip had tried to make Jackson get in the boat, they could have been among those unlucky fishermen.

Thankful dog lover
United States of America

Maybe dogs should be employed as lifeguards at swimming pools and beaches. They would be pretty cheap to employ, too – just a nice bag of juicy bones could be provided when they were off duty!

Dogs are really good at telling the time, in that the daily routine of meals, bedtime, walks, the time that mail arrives and so on become part of their knowledge. Dogs often become anxious when their owner allows the phone to ring for some while before answering, or the door is not opened soon after a ring on the bell. It seems they enjoy a routine and like things to be dealt with in an orderly fashion.

Animals are often great clairvoyants!

Often before a natural disaster animals display odd behaviour, or remove themselves completely from the area if they are able – somehow they know what is going to happen, even before scientific equipment picks up any signs . . .

* 1883, the Krakatoa eruption: Animals withdrew from danger zone in plenty of time to reach safety. Many humans and housebound animals died.
* 1922, an earthquake in Copiago, Chile: Cats self-evacuated before earthquake.
* 1960, an earthquake in Agadir, Morocco: Animals were seen abandoning Agadir before any tremors were recorded. 15,000 people died.
* 1963, an earthquake in Skopje, Yugoslavia: Zoo animals behaved strangely for days beforehand, attempting to escape from their cages.
* 1974, an earthquake in California, US: Two horses became distraught, and were later found to have been above the epicentre.
* 1979, an earthquake in Tangshan, China: Chickens refused to eat. A goldfish repeatedly jumped from its bowl to the floor, while others uncharacteristically stayed at the very bottom of their tank, barely moving.
* 1989, an earthquake in California, US: Cats behaved strangely for hours prior to first shocks.

In areas at risk from earthquakes in Japan, it is common for people to have goldfish as an early-warning system – they seem extremely nervous and act strangely before quakes. And maybe weather offices should employ a few animals on their staff. It seems that they could improve the accuracy of forecasts . . .

Smart animals sense earthquakes

Humans can't sense earthquakes

Dog was right

My friend Amanda was working four hours a day at a local library, and left at the same time each day. Her dog knew her routine and, knowing that she wouldn't be gone long when she left, didn't make a fuss. One day, however, Rufus tried to keep her from leaving. He tried to herd Amanda away from the door and back into the house. In the end she managed to get out and left, hearing Rufus howling and scratching at the door.

Within an hour of leaving the house, Amanda was in a three-car accident, and suffered a neck injury as well as a broken leg and a great deal of bruising. Rufus must have foreseen what would happen, and tried to warn and protect Amanda. Now she listens to what he has to say!

Anon
United States of America

Jim the Wonder Dog

In Marshall, Missouri there is a park dedicated to the memory of a Llewellyn setter named Jim. He belonged to Sam Van Arsdale, who found that his dog was by no means a 'dumb animal'! Here's his story.

When Jim was three years old, Sam noticed that Jim could obey commands that contained words he'd not been trained to know – for example, Sam would tell Jim to find a car with a certain number plate or pick out a person with long hair, and Jim would get it right without fail.

Sam and his clever dog were brought before a combined session of state legislature in Jefferson City to be tested. It was assumed that Sam was somehow signalling the correct answers to Jim, so a Morse code was tapped out instructing Jim to pick out particular people. He successfully picked out many people, including the man 'ladies speak of as tall and handsome' and the member who was not paying attention but was playing cards.

Jim also showed evidence of being able to detect the sex of unborn children and winners of elections, and had the most valuable skill of predicting the winners of dog races. Jim was so accurate with these predictions that the Van Arsdales were sent a note threatening Jim's life if he continued to pick the winners of races.

Sam received many offers for Jim from companies, including Paramount and a dog food company – however, he turned down all offers, preferring to keep Jim safe at home. Sam was also afraid that Jim might be stolen by unprincipled gamblers who would take advantage of Jim's profitable skills.

The caretaker of Ridge Park Cemetery, where Jim was buried after his death, says, 'Every day or two, somebody visits the grave or asks where it is. No other grave gets anywhere near this much attention.'

A dog devotee
United States of America

Clean ears signal rain

Athena, our four-year-old Blue Burmese cat, has the ability to accurately predict rain. If she washes behind either ear with her paw, then rain can be expected within 24 hours. She has a near 100 per cent accuracy record, so much so that we tend to take more notice of her meteorological skills than the forecasts on television. Perhaps she is sensitive to barometric pressure – who knows?

Once Athena was washing her face with her paw, and sure enough it went right over and behind her right ear. I informed my son Joshua of her prediction, and he just scoffed at the idea because there was no rain around. An hour later there was the most incredible downpour!

Athena 1, Joshua 0!

Greg Blackman
Australia

Maternal instinct

My husband's family in Iowa have a cat who seems to be able to predict the path of a tornado before it is anywhere near her home! She gave birth to a litter of kittens in the warm safety of their barn, but within a couple of days she moved them to a barn on a neighbouring farm for no discernible reason. Not long afterwards, a tornado destroyed Colin (my brother-in-law) and Bridget's barn but bypassed the barn which now housed the cat and her kittens.

Amazed
United States of America

Andrew says: Cats don't like water – perhaps that is why they can tell when it's arriving!

Cabbage tree signals heavy rain

Two of our cats have displayed totally different behaviour before heavy rain.

Benny, a grey tabby, from a very early age would simply refuse to go outside on some mornings. At times it was brilliantly fine and sunny, yet he would sit before the open door and refuse to budge. We soon realised that he was never wrong and he became our resident forecaster.

Our tortoiseshell Jasmine had another trick that we took a little longer to recognise. When little more than a kitten, she would struggle through the cat door with a cast-off part of a cabbage tree, longer than she was, in her mouth. She would sometimes play with it, but she always left it in a part of the house where everyone could see it. We thought it was a game for her, but after a while it became obvious that she did this only before particularly heavy rain.

Nothing about animals' intelligence surprises us.

Heather Hardiman
New Zealand

Seasonal forecast

In order to survive, animals have developed the ability to predict whether a winter will be mild or harsh. Squirrels, chipmunks and other animals who store food for winter will gather more nuts and seeds for a hard winter. Moles will burrow deeper before a harsh winter than a mild one.

The migrations of birds seem to include a psychic element, as they usually fly only in favourable conditions. Being caught in a storm or blown off course would destroy many of the flock, as they are already flying to the very limit of their capabilities.

Animals can also do short-range weather forecasts. Farmers knew that it was going to rain when their cows lay down. Swallows flying high were a sign of good weather. If bees became agitated and returned to their hives in large numbers, it was a sign of thunderstorms.

There are countless traditional proverbs about animals predicting weather and how humans can interpret their behaviour – see the sidebar for some examples. The accuracy of the proverbs depends on factors such as climate zones – and, of course, don't forget that proverbs which instruct you to go south when cold weather comes should be reversed for people in the southern hemisphere!

Proverbs

*When ladybugs swarm,
expect a day that's warm.*

*Expect the weather to be fair,
when crows fly in pairs.*

*If the rooster crows at night,
he's trying to say rain's in sight.*

*If bees stay at home,
rain will soon come.*

*If they fly away,
fine will be the day.*

*When you see a beaver carrying sticks in its mouth,
it will be a hard winter, you'd better go south.*

Flies bite more before a storm.

*Frogs croak more and ducks
quack louder before rain.*

These true stories make it clear that animals can sense things most humans can't.

Imagine how different the world would be if humans could truly predict the future.

Would our boss accept that we were late for work because we were avoiding a car crash we sensed would happen on the motorway? Would we ever bother to watch the weather reports again?

One thing is for sure, we would all feel much safer if we had an animal's ability to predict and avoid disasters for ourselves and our loved ones.

The enchanting cover photo

worlds premier animal portrait photographer

Masquerading behind the adoring expressions of our most loved pets are the stories and adventures, capers and escapades that have endeared them to us and made them all a special part of the family.

This wonderful new edition of stories about every day animals is brought to life with the enchanting cover photographs by renowned photographer Rachael Hale. Her distinctive images, famous around the world, capture the character and personalities of her favourite friends while allowing her to continue to support her favourite organisation, the SPCA. Now with the success of this series of animal anecdotes now established in New Zealand, Australia, Canada and soon the United Kingdom, perhaps the best story is that the sale of every book makes a generous contribution to animal welfare in that country.

Rachael Hale Photography are proud to be associated with the SMARTER than JACK book series and trusts you'll enjoy every bit as much these heart warming stories that create such cherished images of our pets along with the delightful pictures that tell such wonderful stories themselves.

Rachael Hale Photography Limited, PO Box 28730, Remuera, Auckland, NZ
enquiries@rachaelhale.com, www.rachaelhale.com

SMARTER than JACK® : How it all began

We hope you've enjoyed this SMARTER than JACK book. The books are exciting and entertaining to create and so far we've raised well over US$105,000 to help animals. We are thrilled!

Here's my story about how the SMARTER than JACK series came about.

Until late 1999 my life was a seemingly endless search for the elusive 'fulfilment'. I had this feeling that I was put on this earth to make a difference, but I had no idea how. Coupled with this, I had low self-confidence – not a good combination! This all left me feeling rather frustrated, lonely and unhappy with life. I'd always had a creative streak and loved animals. In my early years I spent many hours designing things such as horse saddles, covers and cat and dog beds. I even did a stint as a professional pet photographer.

Then I remembered something I was once told: do something for the right reasons and good things will come. So that's what I did. I set about starting Avocado Press and creating the first New Zealand edition in the SMARTER than JACK series. All the profit was to go to the Royal New Zealand SPCA.

Good things did come. People were thrilled to be a part of the book and many were first-time writers. Readers were enthralled and many were delighted to receive the book as a gift from friends and family. The Royal New Zealand SPCA was over $43,000 better off and I received many encouraging letters and emails from readers and contributors. What could be better than that?

How could I stop there! It was as if I had created a living thing with the SMARTER than JACK series; it seemed to have a life all of its own. I now had the responsibility of evolving it. It had to continue to benefit animals and people by providing entertainment, warmth and something that people could feel part of. What an awesome responsibility and opportunity, albeit a bit of a scary one!

It is my vision to make SMARTER than JACK synonymous with smart animals and a household name all over the world. The concept is already becoming well known as a unique and effective way for humane societies to raise money, to encourage additional donors and to instil a greater respect for animals. The series is now in Australia, New Zealand, Canada and the United Kingdom.

Avocado Press, as you may have guessed, is a little different. We are about more than just creating books; we're about sharing information and experiences, and developing things in innovative ways. Ideas are most welcome too.

We feel it's possible to run a successful business that is both profitable and that contributes to animal welfare in a significant way. We want people to enjoy and talk about our books; that way, ideas are shared and the better it becomes for everyone.

Thank you for reading my story.

Jenny Campbell
Creator of SMARTER than JACK

Submit a story for our books

We're planning many more exciting books in the SMARTER than JACK series. Your true stories are now being sought.

Look at our web site www.smarterthanjack.com. There, you can read stories, find information on how to submit stories and read entertaining and interesting animal news. You can also sign up to receive the Story of the Week by email. We'd love to hear your ideas, too, on how to make the next books even better.

Guidelines for stories

Your submissions should follow these guidelines:

➤ The story must be true and about a smart animal/s.

➤ The story should be about 100 to 1000 words in length. We may edit it and you will be sent a copy to approve prior to publication.

➤ The story must be written from your point of view, not the animal's.

➤ Photographs and illustrations are welcome if they enhance the story, and if used will most likely appear in black and white.

➤ Submissions can be sent by post to (see the addresses overleaf) or via the web site (www.smarterthanjack.com).

➤ Include your name, your postal and email addresses and your phone number, and indicate if you do not wish your name to be included with your story.

➤ Handwritten submissions are perfectly acceptable, but if you can type them, so much the better.

➤ Posted submissions will not be returned unless a stamped self-addressed envelope is provided.

➤ The writers of stories selected for publication will be notified prior to publication.

➤ Stories are welcome from everybody, and given the charitable nature of our projects there will be no prize money awarded, just recognition for successful submissions.

➤ Partner RSPCAs, SPCAs, humane societies and Avocado Press have the right to publish extracts from the stories received without restriction of location or publication, provided the publication of those extracts helps publicise the SMARTER than JACK series.

Where to send your story

Your story may be submitted via the form at the www.smarterthanjack.com website, or you can email it to submissions@avocadopress.com. You can also mail it to us at the following addresses:

In Canada:
PO Box 819
Tottenham, ON
LOG1WO
Canada

In Australia:
PO Box 170
Ferntree Gully
Vic 3156
Australia

In the United Kingdom:
c/ Integer Group Ltd
Unit 1, Learoyd Road
Mountfield Ind Est
New Romney, Kent, TN28 8XU
United Kingdom

**In New Zealand
and rest of world:**
PO Box 27003
Wellington
New Zealand

Receive a free SMARTER than JACK® gift pack

Did you know that around half our customers buy the SMARTER than JACK books as gifts? We appreciate this and would like to thank and reward those who do so. If you buy eight books in the series we will send you a free gift pack.

All you need to do is buy your eight books and place the stickers from the covers of those books on the form on the next page. Once you have collected eight stickers, complete your details on the form, cut out the page and post it to us. We will then send you your SMARTER than JACK gift pack. Feel free to photocopy this form – that will save cutting a page out of the book.

Do you have a dog or a cat? You can choose from either a cat or dog gift pack. Just indicate your preference.

If this book does not have a sticker on the front and you have received it as a gift, the person who bought it for you may have removed the sticker so that they can get their free gift pack.

Please only remove the sticker from the cover once you have purchased or received the book.

Note that the contents of the SMARTER than JACK gift pack will vary from country to country, but may include:
➤ The SMARTER than JACK mini Collector Series
➤ SMARTER than JACK greeting cards, set of four
➤ Small packet of pet food
➤ Pet toy
➤ Books in the SMARTER than JACK series

Place your stickers here:

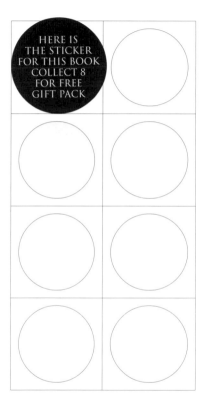

HERE IS THE STICKER FOR THIS BOOK COLLECT 8 FOR FREE GIFT PACK

Complete your details:

Name: _____

Address: _____

City: _____

State and code: _____

Country: _____

Telephone: _____

Email address: _____

Would you like a cat or dog gift pack?   Cat/dog

Post the completed page to us:

In Canada:	In Australia:	In New Zealand and rest of world:
PO Box 819	PO Box 170	PO Box 27003
Tottenham, ON	Ferntree Gully	Wellington
LOG1W0	Vic 3156	New Zealand
Canada	Australia	

Please allow up to four weeks for delivery.

Buy a book

On the next few pages are details of the books that are currently available in the SMARTER than JACK series. To purchase a book you can either go to your local bookstore or order using the form below.

How much are the books?

All the editions cost the same, but the actual price of the series varies from country to country.

New Zealand	$19.95 including GST
Australia	$19.95 including GST
Canada	$17.95 plus GST
United Kingdom	£7.99 including VAT
United States	$11.95 plus taxes

How your purchase will help animals

The Royal New Zealand SPCA, RSPCA Australia, and the Canadian Federation of Humane Societies and their member societies will receive half of the retail price for each book ordered from these organisations by post or half the profit from bookstore sales.

Order online

To order online, please use the submission form at www.smarterthanjack.com.

Order by mail

To order by mail please follow the four easy steps overleaf.

1. Fill in your details and indicate the books you want below

Name: _____

Address: _____

City: _____

State and code: _____

Country: _____

Telephone: _____

Email address: _____

Book	Quantity	Subtotal
New Zealand animals are SMARTER than JACK 1 . . .		
New Zealand animals are SMARTER than JACK 2 . . .		
Australian animals are SMARTER than JACK 1		
Australian animals are SMARTER than JACK 2		
Canadian animals are SMARTER than JACK 1		
Why animals are SMARTER than US		

Subtotal for order: _____

Packaging and post: $5.00

2. Work out the total to pay

Total: _____

3. Choose the payment method

There are two ways you can pay:

➤ By cheque written out and posted to one of the organisations listed below *or*

➤ By filling in the credit card details below.

Card: Visa/MasterCard

Card number: ☐☐☐☐ ☐☐☐☐ ☐☐☐☐ ☐☐☐☐

Name on card: _____ Expiry date: ☐☐/☐☐

4. Send us your order

Post your order to your nearest society at the address overleaf. If you are ordering by mail order, note that some of the books are only available in certain countries. If you live outside the countries where they are available, please request the books from your local bookstore.

Why animals are SMARTER than US

In Canada:	In New Zealand:	Rest of world:
Canadian Federation of	Royal New Zealand SPCA	SMARTER than JACK
Humane Societies	PO Box 15349	PO Box 27003
102-30 Concourse Gate	New Lynn	Wellington
Ottawa, ON	Auckland 1232	New Zealand
K2E 7V7		

In Australia:

Australian Capital Territory	*New South Wales*	*Victoria*
RSPCA ACT	RSPCA NSW	RSPCA Burwood East
PO Box 3082	201 Rookwood Road	3 Burwood Hwy
Weston Creek ACT 2611	Yagoona NSW 2199	Burwood East VIC 3151
Tasmania	*South Australia*	*Western Australia*
RSPCA Tasmania	RSPCA SA	RSPCA WA
PO Box 749	GPO Box 2122	PO Box 3147
Kings Meadows TAS 7249	Adelaide SA 5001	Malaga WA 6945
Northern Territory	*Queensland*	
RSPCA NT	RSPCA Queensland	
PO Box 40034	PO Box 6177	
Casuarina NT 0811	Fairfield Gardens QLD 4103	

Purchase from your local bookstore

Your local bookstore should have the editions you want, or if not, it should be able to order them for you. If it can't get the books, the publisher Avocado Press can be contacted direct by email at: orders@avocadopress.com or by mail at: PO Box 27003, Wellington, New Zealand.